Personal CHRISTMAS Testimonials

Dr. Daney Dumdeang

Table of Contents

DEDICATION

The author would like to dedicate this Christmas Testimony book to all Pastors who have already been in heaven and who are still on the globe, to Christian scholars such as Dr. Joseph Cooke, Tom Atkinson, and Professor Adrian Ziegler.

Special dedication also goes to my lovely wife, Patty Kay Dumdeang, my 3 children and 9 grandchildren, to all members of the Capitol Hill Church, mainly Beal's family, Tom, and his family, including his late wife.

The author would like to dedicate his work to Lilly Cooke and her husband, Philip, who always provided him with information about the history of the Cooke family and also always encouraging him to write about it.

The following pages are a masterpiece of Dr. J. Cooke, Lilly's brother, as he tried to make the Gospel more meaningful to the people in Thailand. It can also benefit to other Christian communities all over the world.

Congratulations to my brother, Dr. J. Cooke.

Dr. Daney Dumdeang

The author would like to give special thanks to his present Pastor, Eilidh. She is leading us as members of the church both socially and spiritually. She is kind, humble, friendly, entertainable, and enjoyable to be with her and listen to her sermon each Sunday. Thank you for inspiring me, my wife, and all members to be stable in the words of God ... she is going beyond her duty.

Dr. Daney DUMDEANG

DEDICATION TO BRADLEY PATTON

The author and his assistant thank you, Bradley Patton, who coordinated with TNB, his team: producer. Editor, for arranging this essential book to complete and marketing for all audience

Dr. Daney Dumdeang

The President of Dumdeang Foundation and his assistant, Tom Rodpradit

DEDICATION TO DAVID BOOMER

David Boomer always encouraged me in my art and passion for writing. Event though he is no longer with us, he passed away four years ago during Covid pandemic. David will be missed and loved forever and ever.

Thank Linda, my sister-in-law, whom has helped review and kindly made suggestion, encouraging my writing and writing congratulations when she knows TBN will accept publishing my book and thank their children and her husbands and their grandchildren as well, who congratulate me for TBN publishing my book.

Dr. Daney Dumdeang

The President of Dumdeang Foundation

Dumdeangrealty@msn.com

APPRECIATION FROM ROBERT DE MALIGNON

In my experience through 73 years, I have found that the Creator links us up with certain individuals and allows us certain experiences to grow us, teach us, and expand our paradigms. Over 20 years ago, I met Daney Dumdeang over the phone through a business relationship. We experienced such a connection, and it hasn't wavered since. We have only met in person a couple of times since we are in different geographic locations. We may not speak for a year at a time, but the connection is never lost. I have learned from his humor, humility, undying optimism, loyalty to friends and family, and a heartfelt caring for others.

He always puts a smile on my face.

He is a learned man who is focused and goal-driven. He is truly a man of God who seeks wisdom from above and perseveres under pressure.

I am honored to call him my friend.

Robert de Malignon

APPRECIATION FROM BOB

Hello, my friend,

It was good to hear that you are using your time there to seek the Lord. I Look forward to hearing about it. You seem to so easily mix Buddhism and Christianity. I feel that they are almost at odds with each other. Buddhism seems to point us to what WE can achieve through our attitudes, i.e., enlightenment, etc. We achieve more internal salvation through our personal growth and awareness. Christianity points us to what Jesus did FOR us, regardless of what we deserve or earn or work for. It seems to me that through Buddhism, our salvation (or enlightenment) comes from merit and through Christianity, through unmerited favor (grace). Also, Jesus said that it is only through Him that one can get to the Father (God). So, either Jesus is speaking the truth, or it is subject to interpretation, or He is a liar.

I am curious how you rectify these points, as you have learned a lot and have studied for a long time. Give me your thoughts on this when you get a chance.

Also, I made sure Pete had Tommy's number, and I pushed him to get going. He's pretty slow.

Blessings to you and Patty.

Bob

ACKNOWLEDGEMENTS

The author would like to acknowledge all Christian scholars and believers for their involvement in publishing this book; Betty Michael, Dr. Yesu Ratnam, Dr. Premanaj, Pastor Cho, Dr. Joseph Cook, Father Richman, Tom Atkinson, and many others that whose names cannot write it all down here but it's will be in my heart forever. In addition, I would like to mention all members of my Capitol Hill Church who continue to spiritually and deeply support me in gathering all my Christmas testimonies and publishing them in the book. They always remind me that as I have already published a Buddhist book, now it's time to make a new one about Christianity. It is a great honor to carry on this request. Apart from that, some readers who read my biography also asked me about how I met my lovely wife, Patty, as I didn't mention in that book. Now, you will find it in this book, as I mentioned in one of my Christmas testimonies. Allen, my friend, found it to be an amazing story after listening to my testimony. So I would like to mention here my special thanks to my wife, Patty, who has always been with me, devoted her life to me, and supported me, especially in my writing career, to my children and grandchildren, who fulfill and make my life happy. Thank God, who gives me endless energy to do His work and to write this book. Now, I can say from the bottom of my heart that writing is not a job, but it is one part of my life.

Hope this book will be useful to you and you will find the point to make your physical and spiritual life better, particularly when you open your mind to accept God in your life. Thank you and enjoy reading.

May God bless you all. Dr. Daney Dumdeang

A NOTE OF GRATITUDE FOR FRANKLIN PUBLISHERS

I would like to extend my heartfelt gratitude to Franklin Publishers for their unwavering support and dedication in bringing this book to life. Your belief in my vision, combined with your expertise and guidance throughout the publishing process, has been invaluable.

Thank you for your commitment to excellence and for helping transform my ideas into a reality that I am truly proud of. This journey has been all the more meaningful because of your partnership.

With deepest appreciation,

Dr. Daney Dumdeang

INTRODUCTION

I would like to express my personal thoughts as an ordinary person who has found God through different trials. I gradually took His word as a guideline for my life and to improve myself as I grew up. I am truly grateful to have become one of the disciples and followers of... Jesus Christ.

This book contains my own experience on Christian testimony combined with the profound educational Bible Verse to help all readers learning and understand the truth of the word of God, which we will experience in our lives, our daily lives, or during our special events which I have already known for myself. It is a given light that guided my life or a miracle coming to my life. I have rewritten this book and would like to dedicate it to all readers. It can be considered as one of God's works, but it was quite late due to the preparation. However, God still gives me time to present it to the world, to our Church, and to all of you.

I have been a Buddhist monk for many years, but since I have known God, he has helped to open my mind, my heart, and my life. I have seen the world differently. God has shown me to understand how things happened. So, I have incorporated all my experiences into this book. Now, it is your turn to do the same things as me by sharing your abundance of goodness on your social network: Facebook, Twitter, e-mail ..etc, just to spread the word of God widely. All of you can be ambassadors in doing God's mission.

WHO IS DANEY DUMDEANG

Daney Dumdeang is the third child of Mr. Khai and Mrs. Intra Dumdeang. When he was young, he lived in a small and beautiful village of Ranote District, Songkhla province, Thailand, which is an independent country in Southeast Asia and has been known as Siam for a long time.

During his teenage, he attended junior high school. He received an unfair punishment from the school's Principal. He then gave up his studies and went to join the Muslim gangster in his area and became chief of the gang shortly thereafter. During his time with the gang, he was homeless until he met a Holy Buddhist Guru with whom he had great faith, so he turned himself into a young Buddhist novice and later ordained as a monk. This time, he continued his study by following the educational system for the monks. Finally, he graduated as a Buddhist.

Later, he went to work at the University of Washington, USA and continued his studies by receiving a scholarship from that University. He graduated with first-class honors and was appointed to teach at that university. He also commuted to teach at the University of British Columbia, Vancouver, Canada. He was one of the two professors of the Univesity of Washington who received a special privilege of full payment for twelve months a year with permission to work for the University for only six months.

Concerning his family life, he married a beautiful woman, Ms. Patty Kay Dumdeang. Both of them have three wonderful children: Dona, Peter, and Tommy. Now, he is very proud to be the grandfather of his lovely nine grandchildren.

He has a peaceful life. He goes to the church regularly with his wife. He then learned the story of God and gained faith in him. With his strong Christian faith, he has converted himself.

To Christianity. He was baptized in a local church in Seattle. His Christian life was advised by his good friend, Dr. Joseph Cook, many pastors, and especially his wife, Patty Kay. He has experienced the power and mercy of God through the miracles happening in his life, which he has shared with everybody and the world in his Christmas Testimony.

Daney Dumdeang is the author of many books, including "21st Century of Buddhism". He also has many published articles, one of which is "Nirvana and Suffering," which he is co-author with Dr. Nicolas of the University of Washington.

He and his wife are now living in Portland in their beautiful house. During the summer season, he usually visits his youngest son, Tommy, and his family in Miami, Florida. He enjoys writing, and now he is stepping up to a new challenge.

As a good Christian, He usually disseminates his experiences in doing God's work during the Christmas season by giving a Christ Testimony. Now, with his assistant, he has gathered all his testimony to publish in a book.

He would like to share with everybody about his miracle life according to the grateful word of God with the hope that all readers' lives will change in a better way, the same as his life after reading.

This book describes the experiences of his journey.

A THANKFUL NOTE
FROM MYSELF

First of all, I would like to thank all models or Christian idols who profoundly guided and led me to become a fundamental Christian. My gratitude today is to Matthew 6:25: *"Therefore, I tell you do not anxious about your life, what you will eat or what you will drink, nor about your body, what you will put on. Is not life more than food, and the body more than clothing?"* and 6:33 *"But seek first the kingdom of God and his righteousness, and all these things will be given to you as well."*

Thanks to Dr. Joseph Cook, who introduced me to the Christian Faith. I was alone when I was a student at the University of Washington. Since I opened my mind to God, I have never been alone. I was better because I knew that He would always be with me. Thanks to my wife, Patty, who truly and strongly believes in her Christian Faith. She has encouraged me to attend church and led me to learn about love and true love. She is everything in my life. As Dona has mentioned on her mother 75 years old's birthday, *"Mother, you are not only my mother, but you are an angel to me and to others."* Yes, my wife is a real angel not only to me but to my children and to you all. My daughter always tells me that there are a lot of things to thank in our life during our Christmas celebration, but for me, a very big thanks goes to all my family members who wholeheartedly encouraged me to write this book.

Thanks again to all my former pastors, especially Pastor Sid Harris, who is with God in heaven now. Dr. David Weakly and his wife, who always shared the word of God with me when he was at the Capitol Hill Church. Dr. Robert Shoulder, who guided me to open my mind to God;

Dr. Bertha Olsen, who introduced me to Dr. Robert; Dr. Chaweng, who gave me time to talk with him about the word of God and also invited me to his church when I was still Buddhist monk at the Buddhist temple in Songkhla near his Church in Thailand.

Finally, I would like to say thank you to all of you who

Somehow, it help relate my life to my Christian Faith today. Last but not least, my special thanks go to Tom Rodpradit, my assistant, who has done hard work in compiling all my manuscripts from many years ago and putting them together for this volume, which you now have in your hands. So, thanks to all of you for your support and for sharing the word of God together with me.

God is specific in the way He is. We should worship him. Even, although He has not given us permission to worship, we should do it in any way that seems right to us. It is human nature to do only what they want to do. *"For the mind that is set on the flesh is hostile to God, for it does not submit to God's law. Indeed, it cannot."* (Romans 8:7)

Thank you,

Dr. Daney Dumdeang

The President of the Dumdeang Foundation

SPECIAL APPRECIATION

I would like to express my deep gratitude to Father Richman, who has taught me the concepts of biblical thought. He trusted me and honored me to teach Christianism in the Department of Philosophy at Seattle University, Washington. I realized that this was the mission that God has given to my life: to be one of His ambassadors and transmit His word to all His children. Thank you to Pastor Smith at Capitol Hill Church, who trusted me and baptized me, making me part of his family with other Christian brothers and sisters. Thank you for your love and care, not only to me but to all my family. Especially when I was in my field research in the south of Thailand, He sent us his sermons to read and to sing together. My thanks also go to Bellingham, who is my role model in the Christian movement, which made me clearly see the meaning of Christianity.

Lastly, I thank everybody who has helped carry out the word of God to the global communities. God bless you all.

Thank you,

Dr. Daney Dumdeang

The President of the Dumdeang Foundation

CHAPTER 1

Christmas Testimony 1979

Greetings from Portland, Oregon. We left the USA in 1975 for Canada and Thailand and lived in Thailand for 15 years. Patty taught English for The Royal Thai Naval Academy for the Thai government. I gave intensive assistance to my family when my father passed away, and when, in 1976, my eldest brother was assassinated, it was extremely difficult for me to protect my family and brothers, sisters, and relatives and also to persuade the Thai government to help me.

This year, I also completed my thesis on Thai Buddhism, Buddhist philosophy, home philosophy, and phenomenology. I lectured at various universities and colleges in Thailand. I was a pioneer in founding the Thai Labor Union to establish fair treatment for industrial workers. I was deeply interested in peasant politics.

We had two kids who were born in Thailand. Dona is six years old and is going to Sacred Heart School. She wants to be a painter. Peter is five years old and is going to the same school. He wants to be a cartoonist. Tommy was born here and wants to be like his brother and sister.

CHAPTER 2

Christmas Testimony 2000

Merry Christmas to you from us:

Time has passed too quickly. Now we are entering the New Year 2001. Of course, a lot of things happened to all of us.

We are still living in the same place and house, except we did a lot of renovations. We built one more bathroom on the main floor, we remolded our cabinet kitchen, and so forth.

Three of our children are all grown up. Dona works at the pharmacy, and Peter is raising his daughter. Tommy is going to school. Dona lost her favorite dog, Mougly; a car hit him.

We have an extended family. Kyra is our grandchild. She is 5 years old now; she is healthy and beautiful.

We have Dee and Sue Jin, who have been living with us for over two years. We are so happy that they are part of our family and they feel at home. We also have one family living with us for 6 months now. We are so crowded but happy.

We have three cats, Sammy, Freddy, and Midnite, and also two dogs, Prince and JR. Our house is full of people and animals.

Just a brief story to you: Merry Xmas and Happy New Year to you From the Dumdeang.

As the Christmas holiday and the New Year are approaching, we are now preparing for the celebration event and for our travels during this holiday season. We also look for Christmas greeting gifts to the people around the world. When my wife and I went shopping in the Moreland area, I heard a Christmas song ... Oh! What am I missing? And yes, I found it, I am missing my annually Christmas Testimony. What's the heck! I have to do it to share with everybody at our Capitol Hill Church. And It seems to me that there is nothing to say more as I have already said before. Well, let's allow God to search my heart (John: 8:9) and let him speak through me for you. This is the only thing that encourages me to be able to sum up and give my words under His guidance. A catholic priest said, and I quoted it, *"Christmas is tenderness for the part, courage for the present, and hope for the future. It is a fervent wish that every cup may overflow with blessing rich and eternal and that every path may lead to peace,"* which is the ultimate goal of life. *"The Earth has grown old with its burden of care, but at Christmas, it is always young, the heart of the jewels burns lustrous and fair, and its soul full of music breaks the air, where the song of angels is sung"* (Phillips Brooks). The morning stars sang together, and all the sons of God shouted for joy.

Man was created in the image of God and given something unique: a soul because God has come for you to be your savior, your redeemer, your Lord. *"And the angels answered her,: the Holy Spirit will come upon you, and the power of the most high will over-shadow you; therefore the child to be born will be called Holy ... The Son of God."* (Luke John 1:12)

Every story in our life must have an end, which is the beginning of a new time. Time is the essence of life as we were born, grew up, and are getting old It is the natural law of change. We say "goodbye to 2010" and "welcome 2011," which will come to an end in the next 12 months. And we will say goodbye again and again. We celebrated the new time last year, and we will celebrate again this year. It is a circle. Everything is in a circle; no end, no beginning. The end of one story will be the beginning of the new story. So, for all of us, the essential and meaningful question is, "What do we do for our lives? What do we do for ourselves? What do we do with other relationships? Do we have for each of us the relation with God's Faith that we received and we have with him? I cannot know about you, but I do know about myself that I have strongly increased my Faith in Him without looking upon Him, but I am certain that He is looking upon me. I was insane and not to be myself when I was unsuccessful in my business, and the national economic was in crisis, and it caused many other problems in my life that was beyond my control. But as I have accepted Him in my mind, I let Him be accountable to each day and forever of my life. Sometimes, I have to live with a struggle in my life, I feel uncertain and doubt of faith in Him as I have to stumble through my life. I feel that I have no objection in my life, so I let him enter in my heart ... and let it be ...

What did I do most of my time this year? I had to fight with the mortgage companies and bankers, talked to lawyer, wrote a ton of correspondences with bankers and others related to the situation. It was really sad and hurt me very much to see foreclosures of the banks to the homeowners all over the country. I try to research on the Civil Protect Act to help them and to help myself too. I even sent the messages to the White House to make sure that President Obama has been carrying on this subject and keeping his promise. I wanted him to keep his words and tell the truth, as he has promised that everyone should have a place to stay.

So, he should enforce the banking regulations. But he is the same as other politicians. He cannot keep his commitment, and he cannot tell us the truth ... he is the leader of our nation. Man has no power to do things only God can do. We must act to God by having faith in Him, not act upon himself. And this is the way that God has encouraged me each day. Proverb 8:13: *"To fear of the Lord is to hate evil: Pride and arrogance."* This says that those who fear God instinctively and earnestly loathe the things that do harm to their life, even the harm is not immediately apparent. If we respect Him and what He stands for – then we will oppose all that He is against which includes anything associated with evil or spirit. I am pointing this topic because God warns us that we cannot depend upon human effort or human power because it will lead us as far as we will not know in the mundane, which is not the superior or higher mundane World since we are very weak as our life is lack of God's strength. We are disappointed from others' promises because we don't believe in God's purpose for all of us ... This is the only reason that all of us should seek the truth, as Paul writes in Romans: 1-2, *"Therefore, I urge you, brothers and sisters, in view of God's mercy, to offer your body as a living sacrifice, holy and pleasing to God – this is your true and proper worship. Do not conform to the pattern of this world, but be transformed by the renewing of your mind. Then you will be able to test and approve what God's will is – his good, pleasing, and perfect will."*

We should realize that the Holy Spirit has already proved that all the world is not right except God -- and we should believe that the Holy Spirit will bring a good thing in our hearts. Without clearly understanding of our guilt and danger, we have never understood the value of Redeemer. We should accept the power of the Redeemer with trust and affection for Him. The same as I do, I have developed my belief in Buddhism and gained full faith in Christianity since I have been in this country more 40 years ago. I believe in the Holy Spirit because He is always revealing Himself in my life. Many years ago, my lovely friend, Pat McConnell, gave a testimony in our Capitol Hill Church with all of us. Do you remember her meaningful, honorable, and logical questions which she raised that day. *"Have I gained my spiritual relationship? Does my spirituality grow more? Or do I gain nothing from this church?"* These questions deeply touched my heart. Pat encouraged me to present my testimony, the same as she does, every year, which make me feel closer and closer to her. I feel that her spirituality has grown more inside her physical body, and he must fully find by herself. The same way as me and all of you as written in John16:13-15: *"However, when He, the spirit of truth, has come. He will guide you into all truth, for he will not speak on His own authority, but whatever He hears, He will speak, and He will tell you things to come. He will glorify Me, for he will take of what is Mine and declare it to you"*. I have to process that our Capitol Hill church has carried on the Holy Spirit of our God and His purpose for over 100 years. Our family here is unique. This church has made me realize that I have already found and achieved the spirit of Truth ... as it has arrived and helped me to see myself beyond myself to see others more than they see themselves. It gives me an enlightenment to understand what the reality of life is. It gives me better believe in his creation. We are all, and all are one because we came from the same origins, that is, God's creation. This gives me room to go beyond who I am and who you are. Who I am is more than who I am, who you are is more than who you are. We are not only who we are but who we are within it ... The strong and solid faith leads me to accept all new things by going beyond racism, gender, religious belief. This is the reason why I have no problems in accepting our present Pastor and never asked who he is, or he is more than who he is. Thank God, we all wholeheartedly accept him as he is and also, we love his fantastic and brilliant sermons. Thank you, Pastor David, for his sincere and honest performance of his duty and service in this church and elsewhere. *"Wherever you are, you always bring happiness to everybody ... and that is who you are!"*

"Jesus Christ will make his home in your hearts as you trust in him. Your roots will grow downs into God's love and keep you strong. And may you have the power to understand, as all God's people should, how wide, how long, how high, and how deep his love is. May you experience the love of Christ, though it is too great to understand fully. Then you will be made complete with all the fullness of life and power that comes from God." (Ephesians 3:17-19)

These words help me get out of my craziness or keep me from going nut. I told myself if I were younger, I would go to Law school and chose a Real Estate's law as my main subject. I would love to change and revise the Foreclosure Laws by giving more fairness and justice to fight against the poverty in this country and around the World. Even now, I still want to do. I don't appreciate or I am fully hate what banks have done to the poor and house owners. What is the good deed that the rich have done to the poor? - No, I have never seen it. I told myself when the time come, I will take responsible to the unfair treatment and the critical mortgage deceit. Then I heard some God's word, which came into my heart that it is not my job, but it is His task. Do I stay calm and in silent? I mentioned this in my testimony to you here to show my connection or my journey with God. It turns me from being worry to be in peace or to overcome my anxiety; finding peace, discovering God or God" 's Holy word, and we can find the solution that God has provided us. God has made the possible victory through Jesus Christ, and Jesus Christ has made all possible for everybody, including all of you, The Capitol Hill church members.

In regards to me, this year, we were able to help one of our goddaughters to complete her Master's degree and return in Thailand to work and live with her family. We are very happy for her. We continue to provide funds from our foundations to help medical needs to one of our longest and dearest friend, who has been a bedridden patient for many years in the Bangkok Hospital. She is now struggling to fight for her life. Thank God for helping us keep our promise and able to serve His will. *"Serve wholeheartedly, as if you were serving the Lord, not people, because you know that the Lord will reward each one for whatever good they do, whether they are slave or free."* (Ephesian 6:7) *"I urge each of us as we are living in Christian life to do our best in connecting ourselves to the great works of our Lord Jesus and will perceive or being perceived the light that He has given us and brought us from the darkness of life. I have come a light into the world. No one who believes in me will stay in darkness"* (John 12:46)

Over family is healthy and happy. We are very proud of them. Thank you, God, we are more than happy to have our new granddaughter, Kayla, our new-born baby. She is eleven and a half months now. She is so sweet. _ my little angel. She brings us even more to be closer together. Thank God Patty and I had a chance to travel to Hawaii for Patty's niece wedding for a week. Thank god to give me time and to allow me to be away from my duty; business and writing. Let me tell you that I'm now writing on

Steve and David' life. Pray for me, please, to help me complete this book. Writing is sometime like cooking. It will never end. But some of it will. It is the art of exposing human thought to the world. I love to write, and I think that it is my life, too. However, taking a break from my routine to Hawaii gave me a chance to get closer to my granddaughter Kayla. We had good time together. We went to the beach, swimming, snorkeling, seeing volcanoes and the natural landmarks of Hawaii, as well as going shopping, dancing, eating out. It was the best time of the year 2010 for us. The trip to Hawaii was thoroughly enjoyable, especially our trip to the volcano. I was with my wife. We happily explored the giant ferns surrounding the volcano. She read the book of Judges and told me the funny story about this tree. When the Judge stopped the fight of fire, water, wind, and mud. I tried to believe her but it was hard to do that. The legend like this story is unbelievable, but when the wife told us story and to be in peace, we should pretend to believe it. And that was I did that day. Certainly, I love the Volcanic National Parks. It is a fantastic and exciting trip to be there. I fully recommend a Hawaii vacation trip to all of you, your family, and everyone who listen to me. I even wish and dream too to have a vacation in my homeland, to stay on the big island which is the paradise on earth and surely it is in Thailand.

Briefly, I am closing. I would like to end up with praying and thanking you all because there are too many greatest things we have done together all over the year 2010. Too many greatest memories in our hearts, too many inspiring, challenging, and unique experiences. We have navigated our spiritual journeys together. Even each of us has different and significant of journey in the spiritual life. Some are welcomed, some are fearful, some has hidden excitement. I would like to share some of my foolish and ignorant experience. The little I am older, I realize how little I knew. Now I know it all. The sins of my youth: stealing a bicycle from the Chinese businessman, selling the bike for gambling and supporting Muslim gangster, and more and more other stories. I told all my committed sins with my Muslim friend to my wife during our Singapore trip some years ago. She told me that I should tell my children about these things, too. Yes, I did it, but not to my children. I'd rather tell my Church people like all of you. Those things are some of my haunting problems during my youth. Life from the past. Why? Because I was ignorant and foolish, I was immature Lord chooses not to remember these things. I am sharing with you, and I want to disclose it here together with all of you. I remember I shared my story with Allen once when he told me about his life that he had involved with the gang. I kept telling myself that it was like my life. I did tell him how, incidentally we have had a similar problem. I guess that it is why we became Christian... trying to completely free myself from the terrible past. These words of Jesus helped me. *"But when the spirit of truth, come, he will guide you into all the truth. He will not speak on his own, he will speak only what he hears. That is why I said the spirit will take from what is mine and make it known to you."* (John 16: 13-15) There words helped me realize all bad things I have done. I have learned and become conscious of the reasons why there are not many people trust God because trusting God requires dealing with sin, now, for me, it is my struggle with my sin to be in peace.

After all, we all want to be very close to the Holy Spirit of our God. We want to perceive the sense of Holiness of him. As we draw ourselves in God, we will receive the sense of Holiness, even it's just a short moment, but it is indescribable. In our mind, we cannot leave without saying thank you to one another in this church, in our community, in our nation and in our global community. So we pray, "May God bless you all ... all church members, families, friends in everywhere, no matter what nationality, especially all who have died in the war for the country and those who spend their time contribute their lives for us. Cheer them up, giving them His gracious land, blessing them, and comfort them and their families and friends.

Thanks for allowing Steve Beal to welcome all of us at this church with a big and lovely smile every Sunday morning and performs a special service with his happy spirit. Thanks God for saving my cousin, Chin Thongmee's life, from a critical heart operation. He is now feeling better. Thanks God for allowing my wife to stay with me ... for life. I also pray for my sister, Warangkhana, who is serving and doing the work of Lord in Thailand. I pray and thank you, our dear friend, Dr. Premraj Varma, who is sincerely serving God's mission by establishing a home for young prisoners and taking care of orphans. Let's pray for Dr. Premraj to have immeasurable energy and solid financial resources to complete this mission in his community as well as in his country, India, and also for Dr. Yesu Ratnam, who helps to establish an orphanage and performs a ministry for all of us. Thanks God for letting us contribute to the construction of the hospital in India. You did all the greatest things for all of us. Thanks for caring and looking after Morgan Medal's life. Thank you all members of Capitol Hill Church who gave Morgan financial and emotional support when she was really need. Pray for the comfort of our enemies. *"But I tell you, love your enemies and pray for those who persecute you, that you may be children of your father in heaven"*. (Matthew 5:44-45) Pray for ending the economic crisis -- for ending war and returning to peace. Pray for all on earth who need to be blessed, and special blessing to our Pastor David Weekly. He is genuinely a man of God; he is the one who God wants him to be. Pray for his wife, Deborah, to be proud of her husband as he has given great service to his family and to all of us. He is a delicate, gentle and polite person in disseminating your Holy word to us, so, God, comfort him and his family, let them guide us with your word on your Birthday. Thank you to be as our own father for giving your life to us. You are here not to be served but to serve all of us, as you said at your dinner table, *"At my dinner table, I invite all people, rich or poor, old or young, black or white, red or brown ... my dinner table is for all of you."*

Merry Christmas and Happy New Year. God bless you all.

The Dumdeang Family Daney Dumdeang

The President of Dumdeang Foundation

"THE LORD BLESS YOU AND KEEP YOU: THE LORD MAKE HIS FACE SHINE UPON YOU. AND BE GRACIOUS TO YOU; THE LORD LIFT UP HIS COUNTENANCE UPON YOU, AND GIVE YOU PEACE.'"

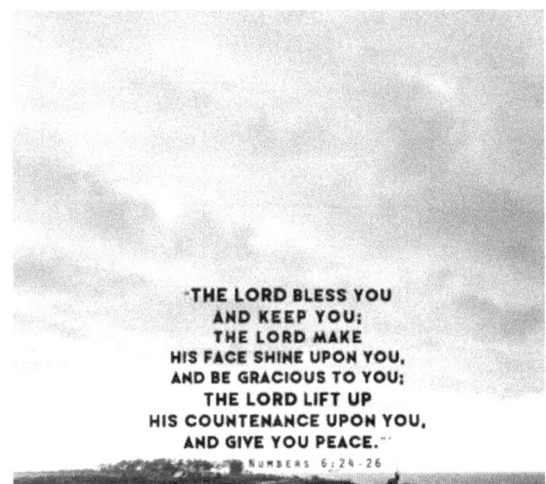

"THE LORD BLESS YOU
AND KEEP YOU;
THE LORD MAKE
HIS FACE SHINE UPON YOU,
AND BE GRACIOUS TO YOU;
THE LORD LIFT UP
HIS COUNTENANCE UPON YOU,
AND GIVE YOU PEACE."
NUMBERS 6:24-26

CHAPTER 3

Christmas Testimony 2011

Why we? Would be blessed

I do know Good. I have been with him before realizing myself since I had been monk practicing Dhamma, the principles. I know Jesus, and I learned that he is the son of God or that God is his father. God is everywhere.

On December 22, Pastor David sent me a message told me that I should share my Christmas Testimony on Sunday, January the first, as it will a be a good day as there will be more people. It will be fine with me as I have not yet sent the ton of messages that were sent to me by Him this year. I don't know where to start my messages and continue until the end. The contribution of God's word has come after the Holy Spirit came and rested upon me. Then, the essential suggestion of my daughter, Dona, before thanksgiving holiday came to my thought. It was an essential key words. She told me, *"Papa, we have so much things to be thankful for, don't you?"* Yes, this is what we always miss ... Thanks to our Lord and his people.

Telling the good thing is not the way to start or to begin the story.

The middle of everything is significant. So did Jesus. He gave up his life to redeem our sin when he was in his middle age. Jesus spend most of His childhood and adolescent with His family doing carpenter's business. Until He was 30 years old, He was baptized and became His public ministry. He gave up His life with His family, and finally, He died by crucifixion when He was 36 years old. So, middle age is the time to achieve life. Look at other leaders in the world, Dalai Lama or John, who discovered Mormonism in this country, our Presidents J. F Kennedy, who was our loved president, or even our present President Barak Obama. They are then all the president of the USA at their middle age. So, it is the appropriate age that God wants us to serve him. God knows very well that His children will get old and they will not as energetic as when they are young. And I found that it is true. Many times Chin asked me if I don't know that I cannot do many things that I used to do ... that may be because I'm getting too old. Of course, we are getting old, and our energy is diminishing day by day. We have to accept it ... it's the truth of life ... birth, growing up, getting sick, getting old and dying.

My love story began in August 1961, when I was young, I was 16 years old. I was sent to do Buddhist Mission in Burma. In the flight, on the way to Burma, I saw an angel, and she held me under her wings. This angel took me to see a young, beautiful girl, and I knew that the girl will be my sweetheart and my future soul mate. I could not believe that the beautiful girl introduced by the angel that day has been my lovely wife until the present day. Allen and Mary asked how I met my life, I told them all the story. Allen told me that my story was the best story of all. A few years later, in 1966, I was awarded a Fulbright scholarship and Asian Foundation to continue my graduate study at the University of Washington, USA. I studied Philosophy, Political Sciences, and Asian Literature. In August 1970, I met a beautiful girl at the Parrington Hall College, University of Washington. I was excited as that girl was the one who was introduced to me by the angel a few years ago. She has a gorgeous blue-eyed girl with blonde hair and beautiful smile, and I fell in love with her at first sight. I asked my angel God this is the same girl introduced to me on my way to Burma. Yes, this is that one. She is the same person. I was so amazing. Since that day, we were together, and two years later, we got married, and we have been together until now.

True love is knowing someone so well, so deeply, so completely. She is my true love; I feel both emotional and physical connection with her. My true love goes beyond anything that cannot be described by human words. It is something touching my heart as an eternal song ... That woman is my true love today and forever. She is not only my wife but also my soul mate, my sunshine, the grace within my heart that fills my soul, and also the wind beneath my wings. Our love continues beyond everything. You all are also a part of the story of my wife and I, as she loves everybody in this church and others, too. It is her nature. I have just known that God asked me to share my story to those who care, and He would like all of you to share your love story and a lot of experience to us, too. Our friends who lost the love ones, please know that the body is something that will disappear, but the soul is not like that. My wife and I we have 3 children, we take care of them as a team parent. We have a happy married life. And I will not lie to you that, of course, sometimes, our marriage life has been up and down as well as other married couples. Of course, it is not always, or all the time, happy. After All, we have our love connection and also a connection on our spiritual level more than a physical level. If one's life has to fight in a mundane world, it's be better to continue his living in the spiritual or supermundane world so that his/her life will fulfill with happiness, joy, and peace. A lover may say; *"If you need anything, I'll be there."* It is true love,

"Love and faithfulness meet together: righteousness and peace kiss each other." (Psalm 85:10) and *"we are called to speak the truth in love"* (Ephesians 4:16) and *"to those who call Him upon Him in truth"* (Psalm 34). This is a part of my life, my memories which Jesus was created. I invite each of you to share your memories to all of us. So our lives can be refreshed and become vital again. To keep love last forever, we must show love to each other, not only on St. Valentine's Day. *"Dear friends, since God so loved us, we surely ought to love one another."* (John 4:11)

Besides having each other, Patty and me, we still have three wonderful children who are all grown up, four grand-children and many God-children. We are happy as we are. Thanks God for making our cross-cultural marriages work well and always will be. God's gift is the excellent gift and beyond other gifts, and that is our marriage life. Happy marriage, one for all, all for one.

And that is my life with my dream of a fairy tale ending. May I have a song of the angel that I have heard it up high one."

Thank God for Peter, our son, who is the life coach for young children. Both in Washington and Oregon and also around the states, wherever the children's parents need as he sincerely devoted his life and his time to the children who need help. As you know that, the children who have more free time usually join the gangs and drop out of school. It is the worst thing for the children. Peter and his teams understand very well this situation. He doesn't want evil forces to ruin the children. The parents trust him as he does his job very well. Thank God that you changed Peter and his life. He knows himself and does his duty perfectly. He has participated in various activities of the club for young people, both girls and boys, for many years to help them create a positive attitude to live a beautiful life in the future. Peter is considered as the rolemodel for children by their parent. Patty and I are so proud of Peter. We fully support him 100% for everything he has done for the community and for our young children. I still remember, on one Sunday, David asked us to pray for the future of our young or teenager after I have announced that we lost our young friend, Allen, as he was severely stabbed and died.

Thank God for Myla, who is the best mother for her three children, yes, our grandchildren, and help take good care of her nephew, Dylan, as well. Because, her brother Morgan is not quite well. Myla gives support Peter 100%. She accompanies him everywhere he goes for his work without any complaint. She is really like our daughter more than our daughter-in-law. During our trip to Thailand to pay our last respect to my mother during the funeral ceremony, Myla also sent her heart to join us in praying for my late mother. Thank God she is really a part of my family. May God protect her and help her relieve her anxiety about her brother's health. After All, Patty and I we feel close and closer to her. We enjoy being with her listening to her story. She is a bright young lady. Her life is devoted to his children, her family, and her community. Thank God that the medical doctor has arranged next operation to her brother, Morgan. We prayed that God would keep his eyes on Morgan and also keep him in His care. And just today that, we got a good news that the operation went well, and now he has returned to recuperate at his home with his mother, Michele. Thank to you all in this church who prayed for Morgan. *"He heals the brokenhearted and binds up their wounds"* (Psalm 147:3). Thanks God for your Grace and care for your children. All of the rich happiness is ours by the exclusive Grace of God. God has a marvelous ability to heal Morgan's health. The world of his grace will able to build you up ...

We love all children, and we have to love them unconditionally as God loves. Without faith in God, who around us or around our children, we can trust. So, building Faith in Jesus is the only way we should do. *"Trust in the Lord with all your heart and lean not on your own understanding"* (Proverbs 3: 5-6). I would like to remind all leaders in our society that to acknowledge the Lord is to keep him in every events, no matter they are private or public. It means at all time of our lives. The Bible shows that the Lord, the man of sin, has a good connection with a large political power and also a religious influence. It should be understood that we are dealing with a person who is the global significance prophet. To me, living with God is not to confine ourselves to worship God, as God has involved in every moment of each day. The teaching of God will guide our lives since waking up in the morning until sleeping at night. God wants us to remember Him, to trust on Him, and obey Him all the time. I do know from my heart that God has promised His children, like you and me, that He will go ahead, lead us, and ready to eliminate any obstructions or danger on our path. For example, the story of Pat Mc Connell, our friend, can testify to the great mercy of God. On Sunday, December 18, 2011, Patt didn't realize that she can enjoy life and has a happy time again, as her heart is filled with sorrow after losing her dear son. She would never feel joy any more. But after hearing the beautiful music and seeing Christmas tree decorations, she remembered the women who made these beautiful decorations last year and all happy and joyful time that she had with them during Christmas Party. Pat said, *"I'm so happy to be able to see the New Year and to enjoy my life again."* The greatest pain in my life is to know the pain of all my dear friends in this Capitol Hill Church. This is the reason why I try to follow God to help people, and wish that people can understand and help others to have hope in their hearts or to shed light on hope in their hearts and souls. Let the dark hope shine. I am asking all of you now to do this to each other. To love the neighbors as thyself, which is approved by our Lord, Jesus Christ. Why? because our Lord wants us to unite to be one, to gain more power to do things. That is what God wants us to be, or to live as godly lives. In addition, He wants us to be successful and have a happy life as well. So we should trust on Him and follow His instruction. He will lead us and sweep away all our problems. It's something that really encourage us. And this is why I have shared my personal life with you. As God desires that his children should strengthen their spiritual mind and developing themselves in being more Christian to maturity or entering the ministry. Each of us can be instrument in the edification process. *"Let us therefore make every effort to do what leads to peace and to mutual edification"* (Roman 14:19) ... *"Each of us should please our neighbor for their good, to build them up."* (Roman 15:2). Normally, human beings are never content what they have. Husbands tend to look at other people's wives as more beautiful than their own. So is the wife, often see that other husbands are better than her own. Why? May be because of a weak and sinful mind, which allowed to be overwhelmed by Satan. So we must control ourselves and should be satisfied of what we have and also should take care of one another. Don't let egoism dominates ourselves. Don't be under delusion which will take over our mind. Lord has also emphasized this to us. It is too bad and shameful to our nation that in today society, there are some people who look at men and women as sexual subjects instead of human being. It is really sinful. Too bad for them to allow the devil or Satan take over their weakness. They should open their mind and allow God embrace their heart.

Thanks to our daughter, Dona, who enlightens the doctors on her new medical finding by using the new medical equipment, which helps the doctors in saving lives of the heart disease patients. Dona is happy with her life and enjoys what she has done. Thanks to her again, as she has helped manage our rental properties. She does a great job and also get along very well with our tenants. She has run business with her heart. Thank God, she is able to buy a new house with her good friend, Maddy which is her dream. And now, she can achieve it.

Thanks to Jan, who is still one of our family members, she has a big heart. She cares to everyone. She is a fun person to travel with. I, personally, had a lot of fun during my Hawaii trip with her. She is like a child when she was happy and having fun. Her character is the gift to her by God. Jan told me that she loves what I said about Myla. And I told her that I didn't say anything. It was not my words, but it's from God, and also, her characters that I have just described, too, is not from me, but it is the word of God.

Thank God for Tommy, who is a good father and also a good mate to his girlfriend, Erika. Tommy has cooperated in a new computer world, and he has created the new X-boxes. Pray for him that he probably inherited some of Steve Job's ablities. Tommy has three children, including Kayla. All of his children are gorgeous and healthy. Patty and I enjoy seeing Kayla growing up. She represents pure love for us. Kayla love her cat, Bobi, so she calls everyone, including me, Bobi.

Thanks to our pit bull dogs, Rama and Boo Boo, who are very polite, never bites any stranger, keep their eyes on our house very well. Thanks to our cat, Sammy, who did not kill any birds this year. Animals are one part of our lives. David told me that he missed his beloved dog very much and very sad to put him to sleep forever. Animal is a part of his family and other animals are, as well.

Thank God for allowing me to be born in Thailand and to be proud to be an American too. God has divided us into different nation, culture, race, language, belief. But after all, God gives us all unconditional love, and His heart is full of love of human being because we are all His children. We are God's family. We are one and one for all. Glory is to the God in the highest.

Thank you to God for Alena, who is one of your angels. She has attended church since she has been young. Now, she is only 7 years old, but she has inspired her brother; Khai, and her cousin, Dylan, to come along with her to the church every Sunday ... So sweet. Thank God for giving her the foundation of a wonderful life since she has been a little girl. Her eyes shine brightly from the contact with the divine spirit. Thank God for giving Khai a talent for sports. He is a star among other players in his sport. He is loved by his team and his coach.

Thanks God for Kyra for shining herself to be leadership in her school. She has inspired her friends to have a beautiful future life. For her, she loves to be a journalist. All of you know the young people of our nation are our future. We have to give them a solid foundation, and no foundation is more important than to be good Christian with strong Christian belief. America is the capital of Western Culture for me. According to my research over 30 years, I tried to examine a classical illustration of spiritled prayers, and I realized that a significant aspects of the will of God involves in the laboring of prayers for Lord and being fruitful in every good work. The abundant grace of God is able to produce abundant ministry in our lives. *"And God is able to bless you abundantly, so that in all things at all times, having all that you need, you will abound in every God works"* (Corinthian 9:8). In my heart, I understand that the core of God's will exists. So How? Via His grace giving to all of us who have faith in Him, know Him and His son, Jesus Christ. Both of them have their life in us all. The fundamental key of our beliefs and devotion is to connect with God and know Him. *"But grow in the grace and knowledge of our Lord and Savior Jesus Christ. To him be glory both now and forever."* (2 Peter 3:18). This is the most vital part of God's will. He is as the spiritual empowerment for us, and He strengthens us with all His mighty, glorious power. *"I can do all this through Him who gives me strength"* (Philippians 4:13)

Now, I would like to share with of you here the thing that I cannot make omission, and I wondered why God does let this bad thing happened to me and my wife? I didn't stop to ask myself, why me? why us? Last night at 12.15 am, shouted one of my tenant that the house is on fire. *"which house"* asked Patty. *"The rental next door".* Having heard those words, Patty and I ran out of our house as quickly as we can and tried to contact the fire truck and related people. *"I feel so bad",* said my wife. I only convinced her that this situation was beyond our control. My whole body was shaking, and I was just about to faint. We tried to check if there was anyone in the house and I felt better to know that there was no one there, but later on, we found that there was a cat that could not survive. Oh, it's so terrible. I imagined how it struggled to fight for its life. Poor cat, Mr. T! And today we found that there was one more cat who died in the fire. Poor animal! The whole night, I could not sleep, thinking about those cats and my property, too. I was sick to think that I have to face the circle of life about fire insurance and the mortgage business again. I keep asking myself, why me, why God did this thing to me over and over again because this time was the third house in my life. And I found that the situation that my house is on fire almost happens every 3 years in my life. If you were in my shoes, what would you think? Where is God? This question comes to my mind for a long time. I believed that God creates us in His image, and He gives us His free will. It's not something that needs to be asked. Yes, there is God, there is no doubt in my mind that God does exist, but where is He when I seriously want Him (Or when we want His protection)? Why does He bother to create us or me? I think that He knows that if He would give us the choice, we could, or maybe we chose to ignore Him. So if He choose feasible way that is giving us the freedom to choose, we will please God by choosing to believe in Him? Ultimately, I have to take a break, stop worrying, just only make my heart believing in God, and He will be as He is ... and I have to live my life according to that belief.

Well, if God loves everyone, why does He allow suffering or bad deeds (or Karma), bad fortune, pain, and even death happen to us? To this point, I have experience and heard by myself. I wondered why God has allowed so much suffering in our life. For example, our son's friend was stabbed to death a few weeks ago, and our friend's son committed suicide a few months ago ... And also, there is so much violence in the country. My older brother was murdered, and other people too. Our society today is extremely deteriorated. We cannot count all suffering in which human being may confront because it can happen and may happen again and again. Just likes the fire on our rental house last night (Dec 27/11). We lost over half a million dollars on this case. And I cannot stop asking why this unpleasant situation has occurred to me again and again. Why it does happen to His children who He loves! You all here, please sincerely answer me, share with me, even one of you or some of you or you all, please.

Does God let the damaging things happen to the good people like you and me? Anyway, I will tell you what happened. On Thursday, December 29, at 10 am., David sent me a voicemail message. *"No, Daney, God didn't punish you, as Patty, and you are good person."* Thanks, David, for kindly understanding my troubled heart and being there for me when I need you, when I got problems. After listening to David that Deborah and him were very worried about us, my tears came out and filled my face. God makes me realize that when we are in difficult time or bad things happened to our life, there are so many people who love us and ready to help in one or another way. As for my situation, the Liberty Insurance Company called me and told me that if there was anything they could do, they were happy and willing to do for me. They said that they are so sorry what was happened and for the death of two cats, too. Trauma Intervention Volunteers came over and stayed with us until the last minute of the fire. They shared their love and concern on behalf of the Spirit of American people. They also offered some of our tenants to find a place to stay, to give them clothes food. There were a lot of calls to offer help and necessary things. I cried of joy at the miracle of love of my American fellows. It touched my heart deeply. Otherwise, I would have no chance to experience the love from other people. Our dear friend told me, *"God will surely work out something for you, so don't worry"*

I told Bob, *"I wonder what God is going to do to me next and what He is going to do with the people who put their faith in Him like me."* My terrible situation this time shows me to understand some of my neighbors better. I was surprised that they didn't say anything or even express their sympathy for my loss. What kind of neighborhood do I have! Am not good enough for them? Or Have I done things not enough for God? Or I deserve no sympathy from them? But where is our heart? Love the neighbors and thyself? Are we truly Christians and practice this? Or do we just say the words? This message keeps going in my heart and bothering me during my difficult time like this. Of course, I am not a pastor or spiritual leader, but I am tired of so-called good Christians and fake Christians. Why do we have to fake so much? or. Why do we spend too much time to please everybody and make a little effort to please God? When I asked myself about these questions, I have never found a good answer. So, this is the time we should decide to stop acting and start doing something seriously. Our choice, our lives will begin in another real way, to be truly Christian. And this is the best gift of all gifts for all of us in the year 2012. And at this point, I understand that this year is the conscious year of goal of continuing to live for all friends in Capitol Hill Church. To me, friends are like each page of my life book. Each page contains with different subjects. But you are my index page for the details of my life. A friend is a friend forever ... Since the day I was born until the day in my graveyard, I have been in the hand of God, and everyone in this church are friends of mine ... I wrote a song after my house was on fire, like this ...

"There are some people I remembered whom I thought that they were my best friends, but once and every time I turned my back, they are ready to draw their knives and slowly strike me. So I searched through many places, after many different faces, with hope for a long-lasting friendship. Well, someone must have a plan, like me, cause when I cannot do, Jesus can! And I've found the best friend I have ever known. Through the valley of shadow, passed over the mountain of good times, we'll get high upon since our memories are so fine and the rocky road of sorrow cannot makes change in our mind. They are so fine, friends of mine, friends of mine..."

God gives the reason of hiding love behind His purpose, What more I can ask from Him. *"And God shall wipe away all tears from their eyes, and there shall be no more death, neither sorrow nor crying, neither shall these be any more pain for the former things are passed away."* (Revelation 21:3-4). *"This poor man cried, and the Lord heard him and saved him out of all his troubles. The angel of the Lord encamps around those who fear Him and delivers them."* (Psalm 34:6-2)

Our God is pleased when we honor His grace and seek His perfect love. *"You are the light of the world. A town built on a hill cannot be hidden. Neither do people light a lamp and put it under the bowl."* (Mathew 6: 13-16).

I am so thankful that God turned my life from the bad direction where I have been heading as one of the Muslim gang member in the south of Thailand. I became a Buddhist monk, and finally, I am now a true Christian believer. Thank you for turning Chin's life and safe him. Jesus wants us to love one another as the unity of love. Jesus gave His life to pay our debt of sin. He is our redeemer, our Glory. His life is created for us. And we will receive His spiritual life. He, the only one God, gives His life to all human beings. Therefore, we have to walk in and with Him. If we have not yet done it, this year, we will do it. We will walk in and with Him. The only way to receive Him is by grace. We must walk by grace, by the grace of God. Remember, when we first received Christ, He was our only hope. Now, we are the people who walk with Him the same way as He did. I believe from the bottom of my heart that He wants us to walk in the path of God with godliness, in Christ's likeness. God works this into our hearts by His grace. The grace of God does not only save the souls of all who believe in Him, but it is also worth to the believers' lives. *"Now I commit you to God and to the word of His grace, which can build you up and give you an inheritance among all those who are sanctified."* (Acts 20:32)

My best wishes and prayers to you. May this Christmas and New Year season draw you into a spiritual embrace with our Emmanuel; for us, a SAVIOR is born.

May Good bless you, your family, friends, and everyone in the World.

Daney Dumdeang

The president of Dumdeang Foundation and Dumdeang Realty

PO Box 2265

Portland, Oregon 97208

dumdeangrealty@msn.com

CHAPTER 4

Christmas Testimony 2015

Dumdeang Family Christmas Letter 2015

Warm wishes to you and your families for a very cheerful holiday season. We, the Dumdeang Family, would like to thank you to our wonderful family, friends, business associates, church members, neighbors, spiritual relationship both in America and around the World. You help keep our spiritual connected strong. Together, we can be looking forward to our boundless future in exceptional prayer, hope, and dreaming of our lives.

"Everyone serves good wine first, and then when people are drunk, the host serves cheap wine. But you have saved the good wine until now." (John 2:10)

December 25/2015

Dear Family and Friends,

Another year is about to pass like a wind and a storm that occur across the World. The year 2016 is coming and our happy holiday season approaches. I begin to write this letter. It seems to me that I have a lot of people to say thank you this year such as my family, friends, and my associates. I am still the President of DORI Inc. and the Dumdeang Foundation, which have done more work this year, both national and global communication services, which are the mission of God and to serve God and good merit or Karma, than in the past. I was honored by the Thai-American Psychologist Association and HOPE (HIV Organization Patience Education). All of these are only a shadow behind God's imagination. My wife and I have drawn closer and closer. We have spent a lot of time together with our children and grandchildren since we have not traveled around the world like in our previous years. The highlight of our life is that we had sold out one of our properties to get rid of the burden we carry on our back. So, there is not much left for us as IRS, and the State has determined that I have to pay 85% in taxes. We have nearly Zero left for ourselves. This country, the USA, with the so-called capital-gain tax, is now killing their citizen. We have to do something to change the Law, not to rip off the American people.

Other thing happened to us this year is that we have lost our Goddaughter, Animal. She passed away of cancer this year. And I had make a trip to Florida for her cremation ceremony. Also, our lovely and angelic dog, Rama, suddenly passed away in ER of lung and liver cancer. We were very sad. And these situation has turned me down. Rama is like my animal-son. He brought a lot of happiness and Joyfulness in my life. Thanks to Sue Lin and Josh for being there in ER giving me moral support, as we desperately wanted at that time. I lost my weight after his death. I cannot sleep or eat well. I still need help even now ... a lot of praying from you. Last year, we lost our dog, "Boo Boo," and our cat, Sammy. So again, this year is the hard time or the worst year of my life. I always miss them.

Sadness still remain in my heart, without all of them: Rama, Boo Boo, and Sammy, nothing is the same as before.

The most significant thing of my life this year is that my dear friend Tom and I have completed the writing of our masterpiece; "The Crisis of Conflicts of the Three Southern-most Provinces Thailand". It will be in the book market by the beginning of the year 2016. This will help refresh my spirit. And I am now continuing to write another books on "Rama, my favorite pet and My Life". Patty is busy as she still be a part-time teacher and help in the Dumdeang Realty Inc. alongside with our daughter, Dona, who manages all our properties. and she is overwhelmed with the work, so we are considering to hire a management company next year. I am glad that Dona and Jen have traveled together in Cancun with Jen's mom to relax on her vacation.

Peter and Myla have their own painting and staging company. They are very busy couple. They always help us to keep and maintain our business ... so their work is very diverse: painting, staging, cleaning, design, and maintaining our properties too.

Kyra is in he junior year at OSU. Khai and Alena are in Middle School, and Delan is in his last year of elementary school. Tommy is still in Miami, working on the farm. His girlfriend, Erika, and family have visited him in October. Kayla is five years old now, and she is in elementary school with Jordan and Jaiden. We miss him constantly; Chin is still with us as I am acting as a caretaker for him when he needs help. Pray that his family helps him more. Sue Jin is also still with us with Josh. She is very lucky to receive great help for her physical condition from the good doctors. She has been refreshing her spirit.

Michele continues to open her beautiful home for students from around the world. She loves Summer like her own daughter. Pray for her court hearing that will be coming up early next year.

God bless you all. Enjoy Christmas 2015.

And have a very happy and bright New Year 2016.

The Dumdeang Family

CHAPTER 5

Christmas Testimony 2017

Dear Family and friends,

I am trying to write the real things that happen in my life and my family, too, as I enjoy writing and love to share my story with friends, community, and even the World. My writing is not only the amazing story but also a Christmas testimony. I dare to do it with honesty, and I am very proud of myself. The things that I wrote is the real thing. I didn't try to show that my family is perfect or better than others. I would like just to tell you the power of God and merit or good Karma that I and my family have done this year and will continue to do it so far and so many years to come. All our activities are concerning the existence of God, that no one can deny as they are our personal experiences with him. We tell the story of our life, how God has worked a Miracle in our life, also blessed us, and changed our life with his encouragement. No one can argue or debate it. When someone share his testimony, he will go beyond the realm of knowledge to the realm of the relationship with God. The Bible says, *"Behold the forms, things have come to pass and new things, I now declare before they spring forth. I tell you of them."* (Isaiah 42:9). We want to look forward to what God continues to do and also the way He is working our life.

As the Christmas happens each year, and a new one in this year, also the new year of 2018 is now coming, each of us should open our heart to receive once again the witness that Jesus was born as the Savior of the world. We continue to live again because of Him, because of His love. And to me, it opened my heart and helped me return to church again after having searched and searched the way for years. Thanks Him for calling me back, I am now ready to serve Him the ways He wants me to be again.

Time has passed by, from moment to moment, from week to week, from month to month, and from year to year, from one life to another life. It's the natural law of everything. So, we are saying goodbye to the year 2017. At the same time, we are welcoming the New Year 2018 with hope, dream, and faith to begin our new, refreshing lives. New goals of our life full of happiness, and our wishes are not only for the New Year 2018 but for many years to come too. Wishing all of us to be able to achieve our destiny, but of course, we cannot do it alone, as God is the one who defines our life, what and who we are in His will, His grace, and His power. So, the way to look back to what was happened in our life during the 2017 is beyond to understand. He is the one who inspired, directed, and dictated those things that occurred in our life. Of course, each year, we have many stories, good and bad, happy and unhappy, success and unsuccessful. It is like two sides of a coin. It is a normal part of life. Let me share some of the events that occurred into my family, to you all, as I have done each year.

One of many critical events that happened to us, which is the most significant and remarkable event that we will never forget ... As our family love to travel during the vacation time both in the USA and around the world. This year, during a vacation, Kyra, one of our granddaughters, and her friends went to St. Thomas Island, a virgin island, for relaxing before her new semester year. Unfortunately, it was hurricane season, and the broadcasting had announced about the Hurricane Irma, which was classed as a 4 or 5 category. We were shocked and worried about Kyra and her friends. We all put our head together tried to get them out of that situation and back home safely. We would like them to go to the bigger island and fly back to the mainland, Florida. Thanks God, she was safe. But for us Patty and I, we have flown to Florida to visit Tommy's family, and we were stuck at the Airport because of the Hurricane Irma. Thousands of flights have been canceled except our flight, which took us out of Miami. But our son Tommy and his family stay in Homestead, which is the pathway that headed the Hurricane. We prayed that the storm would pass Homestead, and our prayer was answered, the storm did not blow through Homestead. It's a miracle that happened to our family. Thanks God, we were all safe. And we are more confident that God will answer when we pray. Since His words promise, *"The righteous will inherit the land and shall dwell therein forever."* (Psalm 37:29)

Furthermore, this year, in October and November, a lot of friends and family members, at least up to 8 people, have passed away. First, my elder greataunt Tep Dumdeang, 120 years old, she lived the longest life as for Thai people. She has been recorded in Thai world history, and her longevity has left as a legacy of Dumdeang family. Others who left us forever this year included Poon Pidum; my brother-in-law, Ratchanee; one of my oldest friend who lived at Phi Phi Island in Krabi province. She passed away during the time of Hurricane Irma, Jaruek, my godbrother, and another one who was my God-son Sommart Boosabong in New York, Dr. Richard Olsen, my best friend in Pennsylvania. In addition, I count another old person of Dumdeang family, 90 years old, who lived in Yala, and one of my cousins lived in the small village where I have grown up. It was hard and hard to me, but I can do nothing, just pray and think that God wanted them to be with Him. I also meditate and understand the Buddhist teachings: there are changes in life: birth, growing up to have old age, sickness, and death, and also suffering and happiness. This is "Anatta or Anatman," which helps me get out of depression and pain and not to blame God. My wife and I have traveled thoroughly at times for funeral ceremony from NY to Thailand, Thailand to USA, Miami to Portland, and back. We both are still tired from our trip to Thailand for Jaruek's funeral ceremony. Thank God our daughter and her friend have fully supported us during these critical, sad trips. We have learned much more things about life from the death of our family and friends. And there is only one way to refresh our spirit, thanks God! For giving us strength for our physical and spiritual life. Even though we lost many people of our life this year but, we have also received a reward. We have some Godchildren into our lives. The more we lose, the more we gain. Moreover, during attending our brother's funeral ceremony, we have reunited with our old friends, both from my hometown and Bangkok, with whom we have never seen each other for over 50 years.

Despite the fact that we didn't have much time, we were able to take a beautiful boat ride on the Chao Phraya River to go to my old temple and to visit my two holy Guru monks, AJARN Sathien, AJARN Ain, whom I have not seen them for over 40 years ago. Patty and I, we have done a lot of things during my short period of time in Thailand. When the time to do things arrive, it means it is the time to do all of them. Should not wait. Life is too short. Enjoy it while you can, while you are alive. This is another part of my life to thank God for letting us, all of us, to be able to live and enjoy our lives. He wants us to get all that He provides us. Thank God for this great mercy, even it cannot be seen ... His power over us, His love to us. Thanks for all He has done.

Let me tell you another story, the miracle happened in the sky. The awful Korean-looking lady acts like she cannot speak English and pays no attention to anyone around her on the Asiana Airlines flight to Korea. In the plane, my seat was by the window, my wife was beside me, and that lady was next to my wife. When my wife wanted to go to the restroom. She excused that lady, but this one totally ignored her. My wife told her again that she needed to go, that lady still pretended that she didn't understand English or to sleep. Finally my wife had to step over across her. Then she turned to me and frightened me. I thought that she might slap my face. When the meal was served, my wife talked to her that the rice soup is delicious and asked if she liked it. Then she replied her in English and ask her that who is the man next to her. "My husband," my wife said then that lady continued talking. She told my wife that Patty and I look like a happy couple, and she was on the way to her sister's funeral ceremony. My wife told her that we, too we, were on the way to my brother's funeral in Thailand. When I heard all of this conversation, I understood that she must be very sad because of losing her sister. So, I said to her that I feel so sorry for he lost. Then, she asked an unexpected question about the cost of building a church in Thailand. I told her that it is about 135,000 US. For covering every works. She told me that in her life, she always dreams to build a church in Myanmar and Thailand. She bent her body for a while then she told me that. There is my 500 US to help building a church in Thailand. Patty and I were shocked. The act that she did is really the glory of God that inspired her. This is the miracle in the way that the Southern part of Thailand is now facing the huge flood, and the churches have been destroyed, we have sent this money to help rebuild the churches. God always makes the way to us. *"Give to everyone who begs from you, and do not refuse the one who wants to borrow from you …"* (Mathew 5:42-43)

Please pray for the flood victims, including my family in the South of Thailand. Pray for the animals, pets, and dog to have enough food, the cows have grass to eat, for the victims to have enough clothes, shelters, food, medicines, and transports, especially boats. Thanks God who sent us the Korean lady in the plane. I don't think God wants me or any of us to judge anyone before getting to know that person. He heard our problems. He listens to us. He answers my prayer, also yours and our prayer all the time. He was never changed. He is always there, walking within our hearts for our lives, forever and ever. Thanks to God.

One thing that we regretted is being unable to see our sister's children: Warangkana and Kuk kai, as they were traveling across the country, another younger sister, Piyawan, as she was far away in Myanmar. We hope to see all of them on our next trip.

Happy New Year 2018 to all.

Now let us tell you about the happiness and positive things of the Dumdeang Family life. We can say that it is a special year for the family. Our daughter, Dona, got married with her beloved and lovely Jen in Tulum, Mexico. Her wedding may be recognized as one of the top 10 events in the world. We invited friends and family from all over the world to come and joy together. We were very happy, especially Dona, that her auntie had come from a very far country, Thailand, to Mexico to join in her greatest event. She did make it happened. Thank God that legally and spiritually, the two families, Powell and Dumdeang, have connected forever. The great thing is that God has brought us close and closer together this year. It's really the special year for us. We can unite the friends and family from three countries: Thailand, the USA, and Mexico. This is beyond us, but it was the miracle of God that makes it happened, daughter, to be in this service.

Peter and his family have had a great year, too. He has a lot of clients, more than he can handle. This makes his financial achievement greater than ever. Myla has assisted Jen, Dona, and Megan to run their business. She is a great mother as well.

Khai has been accepted in the pre-college basketball and he has come along well. Alena is excited to become a model, and Dylan is enjoying his second year in the middle school. Everyone is living very well. Thank God.

Tommy is happy with his work. Erika is a great mother and always busy. We are very proud and happy to be able to spend time with our grandchildren in Miami and to get closer to Erika's parent. They always welcome us warmly whenever we are there. Thanks to the Sardina Family.

Michele and Don are a happy couple. They have done a lot of things together. There were very happy to join Dona's wedding ceremony in Tulum. "I have never enjoyed myself like this before, Daney. This is the best events in my life," said Don to me. It was so kind of him, and I am glad he is happy.

Sue Jin Yi has a good and happier life than before since she has returned to her parents: she does not need to ask for any advice for her life from us anymore. It is good for her. Maddy and Courtney are extremely happy with their family life and with their gorgeous and lovely daughter, Luca.

Chin and Panida are happier in the USA since their son and grandson came to live with them. That was one of their dreams.

Concerning myself, I am still the President of the Dumdeang Foundation and the Dumdeang Realty. This year the Foundation has donated a lot of funds to the USA and Thailand. I also provided some funds to help the school Lunch Program in my hometown to dedicate this merit to my late grandmother-in-law, Pinny, and my late mother-in-law, Dorothy. I still keep contact and work with my old friends, such as Bob. In

Financial Business, I am the author of many books, including my biography my brother Jaruek's biography. To publish my books, I have worked with cowriters; my friend, Tom and a new young godbrother, Sutham. Both of them worked hard and help me very well.

Patty is still teaching at the College as she loves her students and she is very happy to help them. She enjoys her work very much. We love to be together and also with our friends our dogs, especially Marley. He makes us very happy. He is a great and very polite dog but he barks too much as it is his manner to say "hi" to everybody. He takes care of our house. After all, we have had a good year and a good life this year.

May we pray for the fire victims in California to survive from this critical situation. May they get support from all organizations in providing them food, clothes, shelter, medicine and other things needed. May we pray for families of the people who are in the war to save our freedom from the enemies. After all, pray for the President of the United States of America for his generosity to care for his people. Let him be out of the powerful influence of the darkness and engage in the realm of new love and truly love; love of American people. Pray for him not to intimidate of the leader of nations in the world, particularly the President of North Korea, in order to avoid another war. Pray for peace of people in the world. May God bless you all, and may you be happy, healthy, and successful in achieving your dreams in the new coming year, 2018, and forever. May your life be filled with the fruits of your holiday, and can work out your own salvation - the righteousness produces in your life by Jesus Christ. This will bring much glory of God within us. Praise God for doing this. May all of us to be strong to live happily and peacefully and Joyfully in this world with ease. As the bible say, *"And this is the testimony, God has given us eternal life ..."* (John 5:11-12) So let us have this 2017 Christmas inspiring your friends and family with the incredible miracle stories of confident believers who serve Christ in our worldwide community to create and to complete perfect peace in life forever and ever.

Dr. Daney Dumdeang

CHAPTER 6

Christmas Testimony 2021

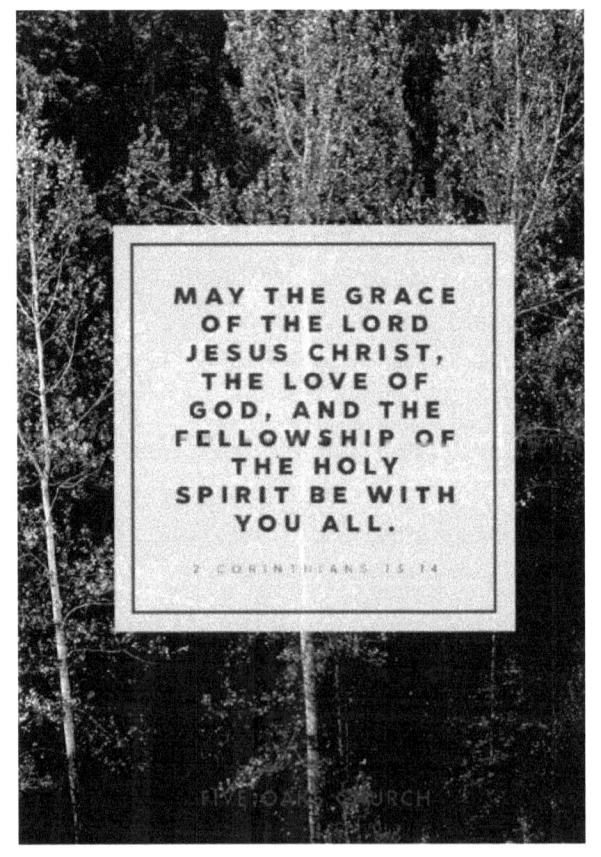

MAY THE GRACE
OF THE LORD
JESUS CHRIST,
THE LOVE OF
GOD, AND THE
FELLOWSHIP OF
THE HOLY
SPIRIT BE WITH
YOU ALL.

2 CORINTHIANS 13:14

Dear families and friends,

As all of you know that, changing is only the nature of life and the essence of time. The changing of life is a part of the human condition, which is beyond our control. But I would like to tell you that I still live at the same address and still use the same phone number.

The following family story is what I would like to share with all of you today. Let's begin with my children:

Tommy is 12 years old now, and he is in the 7th grade at Sellwood Middle School. He loves to read and collect the comic books. He said that his collection is an investment as in the near future, it will be worth over thousand dollars. He is really smart, and is doing great.

Peter has attended various school from JHS. Most recently he has been in Benson Night-time School. He is 16 years old. His life is up and down due to whom he has been involved with. He had an accident last September. Thank God, he is 0. K. He dreams to be a real estate investor. He has a car stereo collection company that he works with his friends. But he still lacks budget. Things are still not going very well for him. He seems to be doing something incoherently, even he is now the president of his company, American Asian International Contractor. He is the youngest president in the country. He was invited to Washington

D.C. while he was in Junior High School. Dona is 17 years old. She is in Cleveland High School.

It seems that this year was her best year. She has seriously been involved in the sports, and she expects to get a scholarship for her College years. Last summer, she made a trip with her sport team to Arizona. She was excited about that. Recently, she has been involved in boys and Girls Club. Most of the members of the clubs love her. Last summer, she was involved as a Junior counselor for Outdoor School too. She loves all the activities she has done as she found that it is a great experience for her. She has her own account and she loves shopping too. She is a smart shopper; she can manage very well her own money. She is doing great.

In regards to my wife, Patty is still teaching at the University of Portland, and she is also Assistant Administrator for ICS, Inc., which has been opened for over the years. It is a top-year work for her, as she has to run a business and take care of her family. She is a little disappointed at Peter life as he has not headed in the direction she expected. However, she often prays for him.

For me, myself after decided to give up my career in education. I had a teaching job for some few years and keep trying various careers. I have donated my time to help the refugees around the world. I also run my business, ICS, Inc., and I am the president of that corporation, which is one of the top ten corporations in the nation. I have opened a Thai Palace to help the immigrants. I have invested over $25,000 in that business. As for my health situation, according to the doctor recommendation, I should stop working for a while. It was a big loss for me to assist homeless or low-income families to live in my properties. I have to deals with various counties, such as Multinomial, Clackamas, and Clatsop, under the Dumdeang Realty Corporation. The first 4 years of the operations, my corporation was doing well in some counties; but it is not quite well in others. I have been involved as a counselor and lecturer for AAA people who completely lost their future their family life, in helping them to get back on the road again. I enjoy doing this so

I have done it intentionally and voluntarily via Salvation Army. Last year, we lost our best pet, Frosty. He was one of our family's best friends. Now we have Pitbrown. He will be 1 year old on December 25 of this year. He is playful and protective toward us. He is the most intelligent animal we ever have. He is Tommy's good friend, and Tommy, on the other hand, is his good friend too. In addition to this, we lost all our cats last year, too.

All of these things is the story of our family over the past year. This is just to let all seriously of you know that ... we are still together and always thinking of you.

Happy Holidays to all of you from all of the Dumdeang Family.

Dr. Daney Dumdeang

CHAPTER 7

Christmas Testimony 2022

Dear friends, families, and relatives,

I have not written a Christmas Messages for over ten years. Before I used to do it as a Dumdeang family's tradition for many years ago. After our Church Capitol is shut down, I was discouraged from doing it. But this year, I would like to write a short message to share with all of you.

During the year 2022-2023, There are many changes occurred both in nature and man-made innovation. For us, we are growing in different stages of life from before, from childhood to adolescence and to adulthood, then growing up into old age. But age is just a number, what matters is our mind/state of mind. Everything is in our thought, in the way of thinking. Spiritual body will be stable as long as you keep your mind in good condition. And in that situation, you are able to do every good things as you wish to do … Please understand this.

According to us, we are living in two different worlds: mundane and spiritual world. Some people live their life in the mundane world and accepts the situations, but some prefer to be in a spiritual world and try to control their mind, thought, or life. It is our choice where we would love to be. All of this is in our mind.

"And let us not grow weary of doing good, for in due season we will reap if we do not give up" (Galatians 6:9)

For the year 2022, I think that my family and I have done very well in many parts of our life. The only thing that made my heart broken down is loosing of our four-legged child "Luk Marley". He was our lovely pet for such a long time. He was 18 years old when he died at the end of August 2022. even he was under the good medical treatment. We tried our best to safe his life. We spent a lot of times and money to provide him the best medical care, but finally, we lost him. I was deeply in shock to know that we lost our dear Marley. He was one of our family members. Marley is one of the best dogs. He has all kinds of qualities that a good human has.

Sorry, let's pass this tragedy. I would like to inform you that I am now writing the book about Marley or Marley biography: "Marley: loyal and modern dog," which will be published on my birthday, January 12, 2023, with hope that the book will be useful and help the pet lovers to take better care of the dogs here, in the USA and around the world. And I hope that this book will be one of the best-seller books like my previous books. Anothing that we have done for Marley is we have also set up the Marley Dumdeang foundation to help dog and pets in America and around globe. Marley will always be missed. We love him, and I am certain that he is now in heaven. Apart from the story of Marley, we are very happy to see our three children grow up in good health, live a good life, well manage their working life and financial life. We are very lucky to be able to see our grandchildren grow up and continue to step into the world of adult. We are really happy to see our last grandson, Varo, grow up. He is now nearly three years old and always with big smile. And we also have more three adopted granddaughters this year. They are happy to be here with us.

Wishing you all good health, happiness, and a successful life for a coming New Year 2023.

The Son of God, the holy child of Mary and the Redeemer of us, is born. May his love bless you all. Merry Christmas and Happy New Year, 2023

Love,

from the Dumdeang Family to your family

BIOGRAPHY

Joseph Cooke was born in southern China. His parents served the lord as missionaries there. They both loved to do work for God with the mountainous people that most of us overlooked. They were being called to help the Lisu tribal group. His father has specialized in Lisu language, even capable to compose many many hymns and songs in the Lisu language, and still remain to use among the Lisu people nowadays.

Also, his mother speaks fluently in Lisu language, yet his father's work still remains to be unpublished. There are many volumes at DR Cooke's residence. He shows the author several times that he is so proud of his parents' work.

In this introduction, I did not intend to write about his parents but only about Dr. J Cooke, so I will do my best to summarize Dr. Cooke's life.

I was told over and over again a number of times about his life, but unfortunately, I never had a chance to write it down as official documents. Right now I have three more hrs in Raipei waiting in transit to write about him.

He was sent to a boarding school by his parents. He somehow seem too close to his parents, but at the same time, I experienced this myself because when I was younger, I felt far away from my parents. I was running away from home and from the Buddhist temple. When I was a Buddhist, who was considered a holy man. Status of being a holy man and my parents being layman made us far, far away. I, therefore, hated this custom. But Dr. Cooke has different feelings about his parents than how my life was. There were a number of time he asked if we can have an interview about his life and go way, way back to his earlier childhood and get to know himself better about who he was, who he is now, and who he will be in the future.

However, a man with his personality has patience, like a gift from God. Even though we never had a chance to get together to finish his book, I know that he counts on me to do this for him.

In the Second World War, the Japanese defeated the American's among. When this happened, he was sent in a ship to Europe, then to New York in the United States of America. He was told that there were a lot of diseases back then. Most of the passengers were sick in the ship and the doctors never knew how to heal them. It was a miracle that he can made himself back to the United State of America and took the train back to where his home town is. His life was unstable. His parents passed away in China, and later on, he went back with his older brother (John, see the letter that he wrote to me) to look for the place where his parents were.

In his teenagers, he was called to serve the lord in the north of Thailand among the Lisu ethnic group (see his bibliography as well).

Note 1:

For the readers who are experts and able to read Thai well, please consult his bibliography that the author has done a sufficient job, and this was very well written.

Note 2:

"The Gospel For Thai ears," given to me on July 1978 by Dr. Cooke, was very well written. He has spent time in Thailand and has experienced the Thai life enough to know exactly what he's talking about. I will keep it as it is because I have no more knowledge than he does about this topic. I, therefore, will go along with the idea of Professor David A. Seamands and quote, "The basic cause of our most troubling emotional/spiritual problems is insufficient grace. It is a strange paradox. Although we sing "Amazing grace" and vigorously proclaim salvation by grace through faith alone, grace is largely head knowledge, a truth believed about God but not a living experience with God. No one understands as a missionary whose life literally came apart at the seams while he was teaching and proclaiming grace."

BIOGRAPHY OF
PROF. DR. JOSEPH R. COOKE

I have come to know Dr. Joseph R. Cooke and have been closely associated with him for more than 40 years since the time I was a student studied in Washington University, where he was teaching, and I was later appointed special lecturer to teach in the same University with him.

Dr. Cooke told me of his story that his parents were American Missionaries in China, and he was born in the Southern part of China. His parents, both father and mother, were Pastor preaching sacred principles of God to the Lisu tribes in China until became proficient in the Lisu language of Lisu tribe, and he also composed songs in praising God, and this song is being used until today.

When he was in teenage, the Second World War broke out. He was taken by Japanese soldiers to Japanese Camp with the consent from his parents, believing that he will be saved and to stay in Japanese camp for his future life.

During the time of his spending in Japanese military camp, he was given the opportunity to study at secondary level. It took years for his parents to come to meet him face-to-face.

When he was telling me his life during wartime to this point, his face appeared with eyes drops because of his lack of comfort from his parents.

Years later, he was taken hostages by German soldiers, putting him on the warship heading for Europe. While being captured on the warship, an epidemic occurred amongst many of hostages, but doctors were not able to determine the causes of diseases and, therefore, were unable to find a cure, causing many hostages to die. But surprisingly, he was safety, and he considered what was happening to him was a "Miracle".

When the warship docked at New York harbor, he was taken to California, and soon after that, he was freed by German soldiers, so he returned to his hometown to look for his parents and relatives and devoted his time in study the principle of Christianity thoroughly.

Years later, he came to Thailand and followed his parent's steps in spreading Christianity, the principles of Jesus Christ, to the Lisu tribe, in Northern Thailand for many years.

Dr. Cooke's greatest pride was receiving Royal grace from His Majesty, King Rama 9 of Thailand, to attend royal meal for many occasions. He was deeply interested in spreading Christianity to Lisu tribe until accumulated the stress caused him hospitalized for some long times.

He then returned to USA. for his further studies Anthropology and Linguistics at Stand ford University in California, and he finished his PhD. From that University, and later was appointed professorship from University of Washington until his retirement.

He came back to Thailand again as a visiting Professor, teaching at several leading Universities, mostly in Northern Thailand, such as Chiangmai University, Payup University, and Chulalongkorn University in Bangkok etc.

He has written an article about his life experiences in the title "The Gospel for Thai Ears," and Dr. David Air Sanmual has praised him: "He is the person who has a deep understanding of the Principles of Jesus Christ, and no one is able to compare to him."

Dr. Joseph R. Cooke asked me to review his article, and I responded to his request with pride, but due to my many obligations, I was not able to review it until I came to Thailand on an official visit to help Tsunami victims and came over his article as to responds to his intention.

I, therefore, praising him in his capacity of the specialist in Thai Language. and at present, he is a director of G.S.M. Thailand, and he and other members are helping me raising fund to support Thailand chapter.

Former Prof. Dr. Daney Dumdeang,

University of Washington,

The President of the Dumdeang Foundation

933 S.E. Renolds Street,

Portland, Oregon, 97202 USA.

dumdeangrealty@msn.com

MESSAGE FROM THE AUTHOR'S ASSISTANT, TOM RODPRADIT

As assistant to the author and as the person who was assigned to write a biography of Dr. Daney Dumdeang, while in the period of writing, I discovered a picture of very old people with Dr. Daney and Patty are supporting him with the older man sitting on a wheelchair caused me to feel that I would be guilty if I would not send this picture to Dr. Daney Dumdeang, the owner of this biography to have a look since I thought that this elderly man must be definitely the important person in the lives of Dumdeang family.

Dr. Daney responds excitedly through his timeline, saying it is a miracle you have found this picture of Prof. Dr. Joseph Cooke, who is a very important figure in his personal lives.

My thoughts are not wrong because this elderly man was someone who has very closed relationship with Dr. Daney Dumdeang for many years, long times around.

Dr. Daney told me Prof. Dr. Joseph Cooke was born in China to a family of American missionaries. When grown up, he was sent to serve as missionary in Northern Thailand for a long time before going back to United States of America to further his doctorate degree in Anthropology and Linguistics at the University of California at Berkeley, east of San Francisco in California.

He was later became Professor of University Of Washington and teach both subjects in that University, where Dr. Daney was teaching there together with Dr.Cooke for many years.

Dr. Cooke was the expertized in anthropology and linguistics and was well-accepted in academic society. He has been invited as a Visiting Professor to many leading University around the world, including in

Thailand, where he was invited as Visiting Professor at Chiangmai University, Payup University, and Chulalongkorn University in Bangkok, etc, for so many years.

In addition to his teaching, Dr. Cooke was missionary leader, preaching and establishing missionary throughout the world, including established GSM Missionary in Thailand and. Walangkana Dumdeang, younger sister of Dr. Daney Dumdeang, was entrusted and appointed as the first Director of GSM for Thailand.

The greatest pride for Dr.Cooke was to receive the Royal Grace from His Majesty King Rama 9 of Thailand to attend the Royal Meal for many times.

Dr. Cooke has pass away peacefully at the age of 80 years old. His body was buried in the Beaverton Commentary, Oregon, USA, and he served as director of GSM together with the author until his death.

Dr. Cooke has created most memorable works in writing, and those who are interested in his works may go and see his website, "Joseph Cooke."

Dr. Daney was honored to draft his speech and entrusted to deliver condolence speech in his funeral service. Despite of the matter was in urgent in preparing, all were in orderly manner and received all welcome to all.

When ending storytelling, Dr. Daney ex-pressed that discovering the picture of Dr. Cooke was not an accidence, but MIRACLE, because Dr. Daney lost this picture for many years and never expected to get it back, and he was excited. This picture was discovered in Bangkok by his assistant, Intarakiart Rodpradit.

Dr. Daney believes in Miracle, and because of discovering of Dr.Cooke this time is miracle, I was asked to write about miracle in my life to be incorporated in his biography book I am writing, and I accepted his request without delay.

Intarakiart (Tom) Rodpradit

CHAPTER 8

The Gospel for Thai Ears

Some suggestions for making the Gospel more meaningful to the Thai.

by Joseph R. Cooke, July 1978

For some time now, I have had an ever-increasing concern for finding more effective ways of communicating the Gospel to the Thaipf, restating the Gospel for Thai ears in such a way that they can hear its message, understand it, and apply it meaningfully to their hearts and lives. Obviously, this is no easy task, for the Thai mind and heart are filled with a host of ideas and attitudes that render the Gospel either incomprehensible or irrelevant. Furthermore, it does little good to try to drive out these ideas and attitudes by substituting new ones that have their roots buried deep in Western thought and culture. But on the other hand, we dare not try to tickle the Thai palate by dishing up a half-baked, watered-down, sugar-coated Buddhist version of the Gospel. So we are faced with the problem of how to present a true picture of the Gospel that nevertheless is truly Thai-one that the Thai can truly hear and respond to.

So far, it seems to me the church (whether represented by the missionary or by the Thai Christian) has not been too successful in this task. There have, indeed, been notable exceptions, but in the main, our message has almost completely missed the Thai mind and heart. The Gospel is seen, perhaps, as something nice and all very well for those who want to believe it. But most of the Thai are doing fine without it. After all, they have their way of life. Their basic needs are being met. And they have their way of life. Their basic needs are being met. And they have their own religion, which, to their way of thinking, is unquestionably better than ours. In any case, it fits them very well. So why do they need Christianity? It's simply irrelevant to them.

Be that as it may, I'd like to make some suggestions here that seem to me to lead in the direction we need to go. And my approach will be first to discuss a few problem areas and then to suggest some concrete steps that might be taken to deepen our understanding and to effect some changes in the way we communicate our message. In making these suggestions, however, I should like to emphasize the fact that they are only suggestions and very preliminary ones at that. I make no attempt to provide definitive answers or even to follow through on the questions I raise. Rather, I am trying to take a new look at certain problems, raise a few new or partly new questions, and toss some of my ideas into the hopper. And in doing this, I am hopeful that I will be able to stimulate creative thought and action on the part of others. First, then, some problems that I feel we need to face.

These mostly concern differences between where the Thai are and where the evangelistic enterprise is. They certainly are not the only problems worth considering, or even necessarily the most important ones, but I believe that a discussion of these problems will shed important light upon the subject at hand.

The Problem of Guilt versus Shame. The problem here is the fact that guilt and shame mean different things to us than they do to the Thai. In fact, it has been said that Thailand (like Japan) has the same, not a guilt, culture. This statement does not reflect the whole truth, but it does tell us something about the Thai culture that cannot be denied. For one thing, the Thai language lacks any satisfactory word for guilt in the theological sense. And certainly, very few Thai ever sense a crushing burden of guilt because of wrongdoing. Shame, on the other hand, does have significant power over people's minds and hearts.

For example, if a Thai were to flatly disobey Buddhist teach-ings by going out hunting (and killing several animals) simply for sport, he would be very unlikely to experience any significant qualms of guilt-provided the deed remained strictly between himself and his conscience or between himself and a group of like-minded friends. (I do not mean to suggest, however, that Buddhism has no moral power to restrain the conscience in the first place, for it often does.) But if the deed were to be brought before the public, thereby showing him up as a poor Buddhist, he might well experience the very real distress of shame.

Furthermore, few would think twice about the possible guilt of indulging in solitary vice, provided there were no external or interpersonal repercussions to his behavior. In fact, it would be difficult for a person to conceive such behavior as being sinful in any way.

Now, the westerner tends to see such attitudes as dishonest or hypocritical. And no doubt, in a sense, they are, but this is not the real issue. The point is that, in a very real sense, what you do in privacy is strictly between you and yourself. If you kill an animal, it's your own karma that is being affected, and if you indulge in solitary vice, you are not sinning against anyone else, even God, because there is no such being. So, actually, society (or other people), with its threat of shame or legal sanction, remains as the chief agent for imparting emotional significance to any kind of wrongdoing.

The net result of all this is the fact that the Thai is very unlikely to find himself burdened with conviction of sin in the theological sense. There is little or no anguish over the guilt of sin, or longings to be washed clean, or religious hun-ger for forgiveness. So, the Pauline doctrines of sin, guilt, and atonement have singularly little effect upon the Thai. They can, perhaps, be rendered vaguely intelligible, but they cannot really be felt. They are simply irrelevant to their scheme of things.

One response to this problem would be to attempt to deepen the Thai's understanding and sense of sin. But I think this has seldom been done very successfully. And if it is to be done, I think we must go about it the long way round--by putting across the personhood of God and by issuing a call to love and righteousness that the Thai themselves see as infinitely desirable. However, I believe a more immediate and fruitful approach would be to follow through on the nature and implications of shame. The first thing we need to do here is to temper our contempt for a morality governed largely by shame, for shame is a much deeper and more fundamental thing that most of us seem to realize.

As a matter of fact, the Bible is absolutely full of references to shame and also to its opposite, honor. Over and over again in Scripture, we meet the experience, the concept, the reality of shame, reproach, and dishonor: Adam and Eve hiding in the garden, Zion stripped naked before her enemies, the goats relegated to the Lord's left-hand side, the guests turned out of the honored seats at the banquet, the solemn words, "I never knew you." Repeatedly, we also find references to honor, glory, and recognition: God's beloved clothed in white garments to hide her nakedness, the sheep on the right-hand side, the call to the higher seats at the banquet, the heart-warming words, "Well done, thou good and faithful servant," and the open rewards for good deeds done in secret. Actually, when one comes right down to it, the Bible has at least as much to say about shame and honor as it does about guilt and innocence or even justification.

Furthermore, there is no reason to think that the ideas of atonement and final judgment need to be opaque to a shame culture. If we cannot easily talk about Jesus bearing our guilt or washing our sins away, we can certainly talk about Him bearing the shame that was due to us because of our sins. And we can certainly talk about estrangement and reconciliation and the price God paid to reconcile us to Himself. And we can readily see that the deepest realities of final judgment are not only matters of guilt and justification but also of shame and honor. For in that day, we will all stand naked and open before the eyes of Him with whom we have to do. The sinner will stand utterly shamed because His uncovered sins leave him naked and utterly contemptible. And the righteous will stand honored, not only as sinners whom grace has accepted but also as ones clothed in new and spotless righteousness that has become their own. In other words, God will not be telling lies when He says "Will done," nor will He be seating blackguards on the high seats of Heaven. The honor will be appropriate, and it will be real.

So then, the reality and the dynamics of shame can be very much a part of our message. In fact, we would do well to really think through our theology in this light. We might indeed find that we could not only improve our presentation to the Thai, but that could come to understand the truth of God better for ourselves.

Then, if we are going to follow through on the nature and implications of shame, we need to understand more about how it works both in human relationships and in the heart of the individual. I hardly know where to turn for light on this subject, but perhaps some preliminary ideas on the subject might be helpful. At any rate, I'd like to take a brief look at the external realities of guilt and shame, and then at the internal response, a person makes to each.

Externally or objectively, shame is the reproach, scorn, ridicule, or contempt that other people heap upon someone who is unacceptable, has failed to measure up to expectations, or has done something contemptible. It is, in effect, a way of belittling or rejecting someone as a punishment for wrong behavior, and it can serve as a means for ensuring proper behavior in the future.

Internally or subjectively, shame is the feeling of ignominy, self-contempt, or worthlessness that someone feels when subjected to the scorn and contempt of others (or even to the imagined scorn and contempt of others). In other words, the shamed person internalizes the perceived or even the imagined opinions of others and, in part, agrees with those opinions. There is, no doubt, also an area of disagreement–a sense that others don't really see the situation properly. But the agreement is there, and it is this agreement that causes one to feel worthless, contemptible, unfit for acceptance or recognition.

Guilt, like shame, has both an outward, objective component and an inward, subjective one. Externally, it implies that a person has committed a crime against legally constituted authority or (on the personal level) that an individual has committed an offense against someone else. This guilt may or may not be punished in some way, but the offense has been committed, and the responsibility for that offense is or should be assigned to the person who committed it.

Incidentally, it is worth noting here that the very great majority of guilt incurred on the human level arises on account of personal, not legal, guilt. Note also that from the Christian point of view, a person incurs guilt for wrongdoing in two completely different dimensions, one toward God and the other toward man. But the Thai Buddhist incurs guilt only in one dimension—toward man, he has no God. This means that, from his own point of view, he cannot even be guilty of a strictly private sin, much less feel so. After all, who or what can he have offended? And, by the same token, justification or forgiveness is bound to be irrelevant in any dimension outside or beyond the societal level. To be sure, Buddhism teaches the Thai that he will always pay for his sins, if not in this life, then in some later existence. Buddhism teaches the Thai that he will always pay for his sins. If not in this life, then it is some later existence. But he cannot be forgiven for them. There is no ultimate power or authority to do so.

As for the internal or subjective dimension of guilt, we can say that this is the inner, emotional response to the external fact of guilt. And when we examine this response, it becomes clear that it is something more than the simple awareness or recognition that an offense has been committed. For when we feel guilty, we not only have the knowledge of having done something wrong, we also feel condemned because of it. In fact, we experience a sense of worthlessness or self-contempt. At the same time, of course, we may have a similar sense concerning someone else's (or God's) opinion of us, but the feeling of guilt is a feeling we have about ourselves. And it's this feeling, this sense of worthlessness or contemptibleness, that causes the characteristic pain of the feeling of guilt, for the pain would be something quite different if it were only the knowledge of the other person's contempt that we had to face. But it's our own bad opinion of ourselves that hurts, for we feel ourselves to be nasty, contemptible, shameful. So, oddly enough, we're back to shame. In fact, it begins to look as if guilt and shame, at least on the subjective level, are very nearly the same thing. Or if we don't want to go that far, we at least have to say that they are inextricably related, for subjective guilt without shame is nothing. It's a shame that gives guilt its sting.

It appears, then, that shame and guilt cultures do indeed have a very significant common ground. We do know the torture of shame, and they do know the sting of guilt. But there remains this very important difference: that for the Thai (and also, of course, for the Japanese), there is no God looking over one's shoulder, reinforcing the moral law and (potentially in the mind of the subject) inducing guilt that smolders and burns even concern-ing sins no one else knows about or that have been forgotten.

Whether or not this God-ward feeling of guilt is always worth sharing with the Thai world, even if we could, is open to question. My personal conviction is that if such guilt comes, it should be the product of a longing and a commitment to a genuine vision of the beauty of love and righteousness that proves to be out of reach. Even then, it does not necessarily please God. Paul opening his heart on the Damascus road is better than Paul beating himself over his failures in Romans 7. But, given man's diseased soul, it is often the case that the latter has to be the prelude to the former. The fact remains, however, that in the Godward dimension of guilt or shame, whether as an external fact or an internal state, there is little or no common ground between Christian culture and Buddhism. But even this obstacle to our witness can at least be partly overcome, I believe, by more effectively putting across the concept and the reality of God's personhood. This could be done both by explicit teaching on the subject and by sharing our own experience of God's personhood - His love, His provision, His discipline, His presence, His fellowship, His call to righteousness and compassion, etc. Then as, the things the Thai already knows about shame, acceptance, forgiveness, reconciliation, etc., can become meaningful in the God-ward dimension. Obviously, putting all this together will not be easy, but I think the effort in this direction could be very rewarding.

The Problem of Making Grace Meaningful. Given the fact that the average Thai is not overly burdened by a sense of guilt, we might be tempted to think that the Good News of Grace would be hard to put across. But we should remember that the Gospel is more than deliverance from guilt, and grace is more than release from a particular theological and psychological experience of condemnation. Such deliverance and release was indeed central to Paul's experience of the Gospel but evidently not to that of Cornelius, and it apparently formed no part of the original encounter of Christ with the twelve disciples. Yet all had a valid experience of the Good News, and all turned from self and sin to the Savior, at least, except Judas. In any case, I believe there are ways that the Gospel and the concept of grace can be made luminous to the Thai without necessarily having to bring them through the Pauline experience of guilt and condemnation.

But first, a definition of grace. And we can start with the well-known definition of grace as unmerited favor. Another very similar definition would be unearned acceptance. So grace is favor or acceptance that is not deserved or earned but comes as a free gift of love. Or, to put it another way, grace is love that reaches out to sinners, to the undeserving, to the hopeless, to the contemptible, to the outcast, to the weak. It is love that beyond hope and beyond understanding, meets me where I am, not where I ought to be. And it gives, eternally, without money and without price. That's what grace is, and that's how it behaves.

Now, it seems clear to me that this kind of favor, acceptance, and love is just as relevant in a shame as in a guilt culture. Just as deliverance from guilt can come as a free gift, so can deliverance from shame. Likewise, acceptance and honor can come not as a matter of merit but as the unearned gift of love. In fact, a shameful culture cries out for the kind of love that is permeated with grace, for people in such a culture almost inevitably live under the tyranny of the earning principle: Measure up, and you receive honor and acceptance. Fail, and you receive contempt, ridicule, shame--- with all the pain, the bitterness, the covering up, the dishonesty that shame necessarily brings in its wake.

As a matter of fact, I'm not sure how heavy a burden the earning principle is upon the Thai heart. Certainly, it is nothing like the burden it is to the Japanese. But I believe it is nevertheless appreciable, and it certainly has significant effects. In fact, I suspect that the pressures of shame account in part for the Thai emphasis on surface morality and also for the tendency to avoid responsibility. For if one is to suffer ignominy for failure, then it is simpler to demand less of oneself or even to avoid the perils of commitment altogether. But if, on the other hand, acceptance were free and unearned, then there would be no need to lower the moral stakes in order to guard against disaster. In any case, since whole-hearted human love is so seldom truly gracious, so seldom free of the merit principle, I think it is likely that the Thai heart to a divine love that is like this.

So much for grace in the context of shame. However, something also needs to be said about grace in the context of condemnation. Here, we must start with the realization that the spirit of condemnation (whether condemnation of oneself or of others) is nowhere near the powerful force in Thai society that it is in most Western cultures. One reason for this is the fact already pointed out above that the Thai has no God to ride him and keep him under a constant burden of self-condemnation. And since he is not himself ridden by the demands of morality or by his own failures, he is under less compulsion to ride others.

Then, since Thai morality gains most of its weight from societal pressurest (not divine pressures), morality tends to be externally concerned with how a person treats his fellow man, especially in matters of surface politeness, not with what the heart is like. And one of the results of this is the fact that the individual's innermost person is pretty much left alone. A person can be what he likes in the inner recesses of his being, for no one is going to lightly break through the walls of his private personhood, either to help, to persuade, to tyrannize and harm, or to exert moral pressure. This means that any condemnation that takes place is going to be oriented more toward a person's behavior than toward his essential personhood. Furthermore, the condemning is less likely to involve open confrontation. It may indeed go on behind a person's back, but it won't be so much the tyrannical face-to-face kind.

Finally, behind everything else is the powerful influence of Buddhist ideals doing their part to counter the spirit of condemnation. For one thing, Buddhism accepts life and people as they come. One doesn't try to change things. One doesn't seek to make people into something different from what they are, into something better or more convenient. One simply adapts. Furthermore, there is the Buddhist respect for life. Each individual life is part of the scheme of things, each what it is because of the inexorable effects of deeds done in previous existences, and each uniquely responsible for its own destiny in lives to come. So, it's not for any individual to invade the utterly private domain of someone else's karma. One just accepts people as they are.

All of this is not to say that condemnation does not exist in This society, for it does. There is such a thing, naturally, as legal condemnation, and there is such a thing as person-to-person condemnation and criticism, though, as we have seen, this is comparatively weak. But there is no such thing as religious condemnation (there being no God to do the condemning). In any case, it is clear that deliverance from condemnation is going to look very different to a Thai than deliverance from condemnation is going to look very different to a Thai than it does to a westerner. So, if we are going to teach the Pauline doctrines of condemnation and justification, we are going to have to be very creative about it.

But there is another side to the coin: In one sense, the Thai already know a lot more about grace than we do, for they know how to live (in a measure at least) without condemning themselves and one another, while we do not. And they already do, in part, accept people where they are rather than where they ought to Be. Certainly, there is a negative side to this kind of acceptance, for they tend to settle for responsibilities and selfishness in themselves and others that ought not to be settled for. But the fact remains that they know something about grace in this dimension that we do not. To us, the spirit of condemnation comes almost second nature. We cannot seem to take morality seriously without going on to condemn ourselves and one another. And so we know little about the 'no condemnation' of grace. Then we carry this anti-gospel over to Thailand and wonder why the people cannot hear the good news when we proclaim it.

If, then, we are to make the Gospel relevant to the Thai, we need to make it much more deeply relevant to ourselves. Then, perhaps, we will be in a position to share the message with them and to focus the truth of grace upon those areas of Thai life where people hurt the most.

One such area involves what we might call the outcasts and the second-rate citizens of Thailand who, perhaps through no fault of their own, have been unable to make the grade in Thai society. They haven't earned their acceptance, so they have been abandoned and tossed aside. I am thinking, of course, of the destitute, the leprosy patients, the refugees, the tribal people. Here, the missionary enterprise has had a significant impact on Thai society. They haven't earned their acceptance, so they have been abandoned and tossed aside. I am thinking, of course, of the destitute, the leprosy patients, the refugees, the tribal people. And here, the missionary enterprise has had a significant impact on Thai society, for it has given the people a picture of what Christianity is, and it has even begun to awaken the Thai conscience. But I want to make one further point: this is one area where the meaning of the good news of grace can come alive for the Thai. They need to hear and understand that God is like this because He is gracious. He sheds forth His love without reference to what is earned or what is deserved; His love encompasses the outcast, the helpless, and the weak. That is grace, and such grace can be abundantly meaningful to the Thai. It, too, is part of the good news we have to proclaim.

One final possibility for making grace meaningful is the area of grace as an unearned love that will not abandon us when it finds us obnoxious, burdensome, or even inconvenient. As we have seen, the Thai is probably less likely than the Westerner to condemn nation as a response To the pressures of life, but he is probably to resort to evasion, running away, and abandonment. If you don't like someone, shun him. If your job is awkward or unpleasant, quit <maybo without even tolling your boss>. And if your marriage is getting difficult, break it up. There's no point knocking yourself out or going through Hell to make it work. The children? Well, perhaps Aunt So-and-so can take care of them. She can probably give them a better education than you can, anyway.

Now, one result of all this is that any given person stands a good chance of getting dumped by other people several times during the course of his life. A surprisingly large proportion of people grow up having been cared for by more than one set of parents or guardians. And other more-or-less serious abandonment are likely to occur. Of course, one eventually develops tough skin and a sort of resiliency that learns to swing with the punches. But I can't help but believe that there is also a residue of inward hurt and loneliness. I still remember the pain in the eyes of a Thai friend when she discovered her roommate had moved out without letting her know.

In any event, I am convinced that there is room in the Thai heart for The good news about a love that isn't like that, a love that won't abandon us when it finds us awkward or inconvenient or when we fail to measure up to its expectations. Surely, they need to know of a love that stays steadfast despite all the things that we might do to fail to merit it. This also is grace. And it is relevant to the Thai where they are,

The Problem of Moral Imperatives. Missionaries have often wished, I'm sure, that the Thai had a deeper sense of sin than they appear to have.

For it seems that people can disobey even the most fundamental laws of Buddhist morality without a qualm. <As a matter of fact, this problem is not all that rare in our own culture, but, naturally, our concern here is with the Thai.

One response to this problem has been to try to get the Thai to face up to the moral standards of his own religion. I remember, for example, how I used to take the laws of Buddhism against adultery and killing and focus them in the area of heart righteousness < as Jesus did with the Old Testament law>. So anger and hatred could be seen as the heart equivalent of murder and lust as adultery. Wall, it seemed to me that the Thai got the point all right and were quite willing to admit that they stood condemned for falling short of the demands of their own religion. But somehow, it didn't seem to matter all that much. Apparently, they didn't feel condemned, so they didn't really need any good news about forgiveness.

I'm not sure that the Thai are significantly less moral in the areas of anger and lust than other people are, but it seems clear that an appeal to such moral standards does little to awaken the conscience, much less to give them any deep hunger and thirst for righteousness. Yet I'm convinced that no real sorrow for sin or concern for righteousness can take place until some moral imperative captures the mind and heart. Where can we find such an imperative if the Thai can look at their own moral standard without being significantly moved?

Well, as it happens, I think there is one aspect of their own standards to which they are already sensitive or could fairly become so. That Is Buddhist ideals. And for another, compassion is by its very nature the Kind of thing that can touch the heart. In fact, as we have seen, this is One area where the Christian message and example have already had a significant impact on Thai land. And it has awakened the conscience more than Anything else the missionary has done. It seems to me, therefore, that the call to compassion could well form The focus of our teaching and example concerning Christian morality. Not That the sterner virtues should be ignored, but even here, the long way around May by the quickest way home. For the heart of even the sterner virtues is love, and once compassion has on the heart's allegiance, the steamer claims of love may have a better chance to win a hearing. So, I feel we should press the claims of compassion even more effectively and intensively than we have in the past. This will continue to involve the demonstration of compassion, of course, but I think it should also involve teaching on compassion as it relates to the Christian doctrine of grace - God's unearned compassion to us and our unearned compassion to others. And behind our teaching on compassion, there should always be the call to commitment, for talking about compassion and occasionally obeying an impulse toward compassionate deeds is not at all the same thing as committing oneself to learning true heart compassion as a way of life.

For the non-Christian, this focus on compassion could accomplish several things. It could make the gospel of grace more meaningful; it could even make the personhood of God more real to him. And if it awakens his conscience to true commitment, it could very well lead to a deeper realization of moral weakness and the need for divine help. Then, for the Christian, it could lead to a much deeper appreciation for God's compassion, to a better understanding of the Christian life, and to a more effective witness.

Concerning the more general problem of moral imperatives, one aspect of the Thai situation is worth noting; the fact that the monks (as one might expect) take morality more seriously than the population as a whole. Now, it is true that the monk is very much concerned with the duty of abiding by the external rules of his order, but this is by no means the whole picture. He is also committed to sexual morality (meaning strict celibacy) and to the control of other passions such as anger, impatience, greed, etc. And I'm sure that compassion is also important. In fact, it 's my impression that monks are held to a fairly high level of morality and self-control, both on account of their own standards and because of the expectations of society in general. It seems likely, therefore, that a great many monks would be hurting on account of the performance gap, the gap between the behavior they expect of themselves and the behavior they are able to produce. I do not actually know that this is indeed the case, but such is my surmise. I have heard, however, that a distressingly large number of monks suffer from emotional breakdowns, and this just might be a symptom of difficulty with the performance gap. At any rate, if my surmise is correct, there must be thousands of monks who might find that the Christian message of grace is very relevant to their needs, for I don't think Buddhism has very much help for those who are struggling with the performance gap. How to meet their needs, though, is another question, for we cannot afford to be either subversive or arrogant about it.

Another segment of Thai society worth mentioning here is those who have left monkhood after being monks for a period of a number of years. Such people have imbibed many of the values of the temple, but at the same time, life in the temple has left them ill-equipped to handle the pressures of everyday life, working, supporting themselves, managing a household, and building fruitful relationships as husbands and fathers. So these men will possibly be suffering from a double dose of the performance gap, first on account of the temple standards of morality and second on account of the daily demands of a life they don't know how to live. Here, then, is one group of people who might well find the Gospel relevant to their needs.

The Problem of Ultimate Reality. Concerning this problem, Christians need to understand that, for the Buddhists, the ultimate reality is impersonal. But at the same time, it is moral. And, furthermore, it is inexorable. In other words, the universe, the whole scheme of things, operates on the basis of inherent moral laws that function remorselessly and inevitably. And at the root of these laws is the fact that every living being (whether god or devil, human, animal, or insect) must invariable reap what it sows. If you do evil, you reap evil (or suffering); if you do good, you reap good. Now, of course, we all know that some people appear to get away with doing wrong, and others appear to suffer even though they do good. But sooner or later, if not in this life, then in another incarnation, or even after hundreds of them, the payoff comes. And it comes without fail, precisely measured to the deed that produced it. Nor is any supreme being needed to see that it happens, for it happens by the very nature of things, just as when one billiard ball strikes another, the reaction of the second ball must be precisely equal to the action of the first. In fact, whatever gods there may be, their deeds are immutably subject to the same laws. There is nothing we or they can do to circumvent it. (it would be a moral outrage if they could) There is no possibility of reprieve. And there is no forgiveness is by its very nature impossible. You might as well ask a stone to forgive you when you stub your toe against it or apologize to the law of gravity when you flout it by jumping off a cliff. The only thing you can possibly do to improve your situation is to store up good deeds to balance the bad.

One obvious result of all this is the fact that sin must have a completely different meaning to the Buddhist than to the Christian. Sin is real to the Buddhist, to be sure, and it has consequences. But ultimately, there is nothing personal about it. (It becomes personal, of course, at the societal level, but this personal aspect is derived, temporal, and is not at all the essential characteristic of sin when seen in its religious dimension.) So, there can be no such thing as ultimate guilt, condemnation, or forgiveness. There are only impersonal consequences.

I suspect, however, that there are other important results of this impersonality. For one thing, I cannot help but believe that the consequences of sin, though firmly believed in, must have an unreal element. For the payoff is so distant, and when it does come, one is unlikely to have any real memory of the sins that brought it, just as in the present life, we have little or no knowledge of the sins that brought about our present miseries.

Secondly, the impersonality of morality would tend, I think, to make one's moral accountability a strictly individual affair. If I sin, it's none of your business. After all, I'm the one that has to pay the piper. And if you happen to get hurt in the process, you probably had it coming because of some sin committed in a previous existence. (I doubt whether any good Buddhist teacher would settle for such reasoning, but it might be a powerful motivating factor for all that.)

Now, as I have already mentioned, there is a personal element to Thai morality, a sphere where the experiences of acceptance, rejection, shame, honor, condemnation, and forgiveness have relevance. And that element, that sphere, is to be found in the framework of society and in the context of relationships with other people. Here, there is occasion for responsible behavior, fair play, consideration for others, compassion, or, conversely for, irresponsibility, dishonesty, and selfishness. Furthermore, Buddhism clearly enjoins certain types of behavior and forbids others. But since ultimate religious accountability is both impersonal and distant, it is easy to slip into a kind of morality where misbehavior only matters if one gets caught. For the Thai have no God who sees all and who necessarily has an opinion, moment by moment, concerning every deed, work, and thought.

At this point, it seems to me we are down to rock-bottom differences between Buddhism and Christianity. Their ultimate reality is impersonal, and ours is personal. And the personhood of God lies at the very center of everything we want to say, whether it be about guilt or shame, justification or honor, condemnation or abandonment, sin or salvation, law or grace. We, therefore, have no option but to try to make the personhood of God meaningful to our Thai audience. Actually, I'm sure missionaries and Thai Christian leaders have been doing this all along, but I believe we should make a more conscious and concerted effort to be more effective in this area. The following suggestions may prove helpful in this regard;

1. Emphasize God's personhood in creation. His will chooses. His wisdom plans. His voice speaks. His power effects. His love seeks fellowship with man whom He creates... I'm afraid I don't have too clear a picture of the specific problems of making creation real to the Thai, but I have no doubt that this needs to be done, and I am sure there are those who can share their experience and wisdom in this area.

2. Make use of the realities of human relationships in Thai society and bring insights from this area to bear on our talk about God. This would involve getting to know and understand the dynamics of shame and honor, criticism and praise, offense and apology, repentance and forgiveness, estrangement and reconciliation, crime and punishment, evasion and accountability, isolation and togetherness, abandonment and persevering love, selfishness and compassion. Then, it would involve developing analogies between

the above human experiences and our relationship with God. This would not necessarily convince the Thai that there is such a thing as a personal God, but at least it could make the teaching about God come alive to him. In any case, the Thai is used to thinking in terms of the existence of all kinds of spirits. And gods inhabiting the universe, and all of these have a personality of a kind. So, the meaning of God's existence and presence could make sense to him, and that is half the battle.

3. Demonstrate a personal relationship with God. This should not be an artificial, preachy thing but a sharing of one's own experience of God with those who are ready to hear. Most important here, I think, is a kind of transparency where we can be seen as what we are, with all our weaknesses, failures, sins, hopes, and aspirations, living with a God who continues to be totally for us and to love us just as we are. This is, perhaps, the very best way we have of sharing the meaning of the good news of grace to others.

Other Problems. The above deals with the chief problems I have on my mind, but obviously, there are others worthy of consideration. These would include the problem of growing materialism in Thai society, the problem of new tensions in the home as the Thai increasingly shift from the extended to the nuclear family structure, the position of the pastor in a society where the role of the religious professional is defined in non-Biblical ways; and many others. One problem that might prove highly significant is the problem of the other-worldliness of Buddhism. This is a problem which is already producing tensions, I believe, in Thai society. In fact, I gather that Buddhism in Thailand is itself undergoing what almost amounts to a crisis of relevance on how to make the religious values of Buddhism relevant to the common man personally, socially, and politically. And religious leaders have arisen in Thailand who are having a real impact in these matters. According to one knowledgeable scholar of my acquaintance, and practical revival will completely change both Buddhism and Thai society, provided that the political situation allows breathing space for such developments. This is a matter well worth further investigation. But I leave these and other such matters aside and conclude with some suggestions for integrating the things I have discussed (as well as other equally relevant issues) into some kind of strategy of evangelism.

Suggestions for strategy Development.

In view of the problems I have discussed and of others that may be equally important, I should like to see some concerted effort made to work through such problems and to plan a strategy of evangelism that might prove more effective for reaching the Thai mind and heart. To this end, I should like to propose the following suggestions. It may be that my suggestions are over-ambitious or over-idealistic, but at least I'd like to set them forth for what they may be worth.

1. Set up a forum for the exchange of ideas. At the very least, this could involve an exchange of letters and papers between those interested. But I'd also like to see arrangements made for an intensive brain-storming session. And I suppose it would help if we could have some kind of standing committee to work with planning, mailing lists, communication, etc. And possibly there would be value in planning a general conference for Christian leaders and workers in Thailand. Whatever we do in the area of setting up a forum could then lead to some of the other possibilities outlined below.

2. Develop a program of research in critical areas. I hope, if nothing else, that my discussion of critical problems above has served to show that there is much that we need to know about Thai society before we can develop a truly relevant approach toward presenting the Gospel. Some of the necessary knowledge is already available to anyone who has lived in Thailand for any length of time with his eyes and ears open. But, other types of knowledge can only be gained through careful research. Some subjects worth researching are the theology of shame, the psychological and social dynamics of shame, the other-worldliness of Buddhism and resulting tensions in Thai personality and society, psychological and religious pressures upon monks and their response to those pressures, the Thai definition of the good man, including consideration of the gaps in their definition and the tensions and dislocations caused by those

gaps; signs of Buddhist revival in Thailand, with consideration of implications and prospects; and so forth.

3.   Develop some concrete suggestions for the possible content and emphases of a Thai-oriented approach to the Gospel and spiritual truth. This would involve working through some of the problems I have discussed, As well as other problems that might emerge, and proposing ways of integrating Our growing understanding into a practical approach for sharing the Gospel. This might even involve preparing a booklet on effective ways of Witnessing to the Thai. But presumably, the "effective ways" would have to Be tested first.

4.   Develop a strategy for orienting Christian workers and missionaries toward a more effective style of witnessing. Such a strategy could involve conferences and workshops also, the preparation and dissemination and dissemination of written materials, input into orientation programs for new missionaries, and teaching and counseling for missionaries on the field, especially with a view to providing insight and help for those dealing with the condemnation pressures so endemic in western Christian subcultures.

5.   Develop a strategy for focusing our witness where it will do the Most good. We are reaching the down-and-outs reasonably well. Is there Some way we can reach into the main body society? And what about The spiritual hunger of monks and of those fresh out of a long stint in the Temple? How can such people best be reached? And by whom?

This is as far as I wish to carry my discussion here. But in closing, I should Like to emphasize once more the exploratory of my paper. What I present is not definitive answers but questions and some suggestions as to where I think answers might be found. However, I do hope for at least Two results from what I have written. One is the beginning of an exchange of ideas between those who are interested in these issues. And the other Is the possibility that more capable and well-informed leaders and thinkers will pick up the ball and run with it. If either of these results emerge, I will be well repaid for my efforts.

CHAPTER 9

Christian Worship

November 22/04 Worship

At this point in the service, a voice cries out, "Let us pray."

The Worshippers now turn to the future tasks of respond suability in and for the world:

December 01/04 at 7:46

My daughter was tired and took time off to sleep in our resort hotel. My wife and I took a taxi to the movement teacher conference as we were invited as distinguished guests:

There are about over thousand audiences and over a hundred movement authorities and so forth:

The conference for training and giving teacher certificates was one of many programs of Villager education that I was personally involved finally and oversee the business plan project. My adder to then like this; Dear my brother as and sisters; GSM associated government authority and young girls land young men ... and whom in the conference: I am so happy to be part of this meeting, I love Tagolu language even I did not know, but I love the way the people pronounce and create sounds, I wished I would know it. I know only sanskrit and Pali. It is better for me today to speak to you in English language since I have the best interpreter on the site, I love this country even I was not born here, but my soul, my heart, and my mind is here. It seem like I was born here, this country is my land, my country, and my holiday and, therefore

I will all do a such hospital project, homes house, and AR House, included education project, I spending my own fund to help the people here, and yet this village is too small compare to other part of the world. Here is my book. It is original copy with 15 dollars, but I will sale in the different campus and v-book marketing industry for $36-5 ($35x60 Indian rope). Let say one million was sold, than we have more fund than we needs to accomplish our project, not only me can do that, but you, as the local here, give the hand and time, and heart together we can do it, as the US president Regan aid together we could make it, and we makes the entirely world knows us from the smallest villager, and from what we did and inform our follower men and women via my book. Then all the world will know and will give us support ... so let pray to have positive thought with our mighty God, let everything in the hand of our Cod, not us we, and only we alone, will not ever get the job done but with Him us and His order to do that job, we will done in his own way...

My wife said this kinds of project is similar to what she is doing in America I then asked my wife to take over (every stand up and clapped their hand so loudly for me and my wife): My wife introduced herself and said she was so happy for this trip and it is special trip for her and she was so happy to be part of educational project which her husband started it to trained teachers and other projects, I (she) always supporting my husband, because he is taking the over from he mighty God not from himself, and even now we even put our own home in the financial market to complete project, I enjoyed to see all teachers, government workers, and GSM associated partner here having strong faith in God, keep doing what we are doing with supporting of my husband and government of India the job will be done. Thanks, we have to go because our daughter is so worried where we are now. And we have to got take her for late late luncheon. Thanks, you and God Bless you and bye-bye for now, crow is chearfully, clap the hands, and they are so happy we left the meeting and back to hotel take a nap:

November 30/04 at 8:05

This is the rerecord of my 2003 trip to India: As soon as I completed my mission of the northern Thailand and Burma as I used to do dues to my promise with my dear friends, we promised to work to gather to help our follower and our community in the nation as well as other nations ... of cause I have done my personal family duty as I usually token did, took before leaving to India.

I took this airline to Chain Nia and my dear friend Dr. Yesu, who I was feel lose when he was in America and our member of GSM and the Mission of God as the whole ... we have similarity ideal, and we are exchanged such a pure and innocents idea of but Buddhism and Christianly. It took us together as brother-hood. Before this trip,, we were student and teacher and hippy in India because I got lost and lost no direction with any kind of what is an accident condition for ... the instance and wise dome that God gives me it will be way beyond and I was taken from there and live my life and hiding my life the Thais gov, thought I was death because I didn't communicate with any of them, I met too many kinds of people from around the world we spokee in different language and we sharing to many storys but in the commend that we are boarding with the world and want some cineaste and better so we are vegetation we thinks we can eat and live by sharing what each of us has for eating we sharing our journey ... around Himalayan hillside, most of them said hey Daney you must each us palms try and an trilogy you are the man can show us the way we are loosing I said I lost too you are not I am not any boy but Thai happy ... one girl from Japan felt close to me and she express her love to me I was so shame and went away from her ... again and again those similarity of situation kept repeatedly. The last one was the German girl. She said she saw something special in me she wanted to spend the rest of her life with me. I will reply the same again and again I have to escape myself from her. She scared me as I'm afraid of falling in love. I didn't even know myself what is love means to me ... we are friends. Daily, we sharing every thing we have, but I feels that I am one of the hippy group and no love involving. But you know I love India. Why? Because India is the motherland of Thai cultural art, I feel than I'm waiting for my mother land and God's work and Buddha's teachings. My dream then is to seek later the inland learning. He, Dr. Yesu, called taxi to take me to small home call army salvation, he was so happy to see me. He asked me if I have army name, that was occurred in the book record of Army salvation. I took cold shower and hurry up to catch the train to Canada ... before I took the train in the Latinate that invite, I was all of the poorest, the oldest, both man and but you gang. I feel so bad I said hey, one $ is 60RP. Why don't give them away for their food or other etc? I did give on by once, and they were following me and told me God Bless you, Guru I am not the guru, but my love to them, my sympathy I have to them ... newspaper such as India in expressed said Guru give million rupee to the homeless, another news Gule of Paper said the Kindly man from USA who was born in Thailand, following the path's of God an Buddha, gave million rupees away ... whatever they stated in the news-paper I was careless because I am who I am. As soon as we arrived, I told Dr. Yesu's son ... he was Bharman, Hindu (see in my book), to pick us after we took 13 hours in the train. He gave the nice and warm welcome and put me in the most beautiful hotel where a Hindu man, Chechen, his friend, is the owner.

He welcomed me and said that he had seen my picture in the newspaper. It is a blessing that I have been there. And again, he welcome the town. He told me that if there was anything I wanted him to do ... please tell him. He also told me that he knew that I was building a hospital and home for homeless children in the village (see the map). He said he was so impressed. "YOU ARE NOT EVEN Indian. Why do you do this? I said, "Yes, I am Indian, and this is my land and my Homeland, too."

Another next day, I was taken to the Village. My picture was there. Ton of crowd were there, they thank you for seeing me in per-son. They were so happy, blessing me, and thankful to me that I am a part and key man to do the necessary project for them. I knows that it was not my intentional but HIS, My Name Daney Dumdeang; I was here at the banner a few years ago. My wife and I came here quite often three years ago when we were in Singapore. Oneday I bought the airline ticket we were just about on the plane when we got a call said that our flight was cancel. My wife was so pumped when she hurt that we had to go to India because our fight was canceled. We were both in silence, and we did not make it. Now I am alone without my wife among the crowd who told me to bring my wife next time. I agreed and promised to bring her with me next time. Before leaving then, they told me to claim and stay that in their home next time. I said yes. I told them they are economically may be poor, but they are rich in Faith of God. They were so happy. I continue my talk that I was called to be here and promised to complete the hospital base under His authority, not mine. I have to take in account and could not help but continue His Mission because His spirit tell me to do. I beg God for years that he would never stop me to serve Him and let Him guide me what to do, and I will follow Him. Here I am and, participate as the partner-ship with Him like all my brother and sister around the world. I saw a million of face filled with hope, and that reflect the great mission such as the one of Mother Theresa. "who I am", I often ask myself when I was young. I am the man of God, or I am His returnee, what and why He did, what He did to me and His follower ... etc ... with my two eyes, I see His great mercy, entered to my mind and my heart. The Word of God must go forth ... I believe you will understand the loneliness that calls you in to the great love and why? I am here to respond to your needs. With my association GSM and partnership with God, I will continue to completed this project for the community and for you all. I have to stop now as I am so tired from a long trip, but I will continue my talk again tomorrow.

November 29/04 at 8:02:

BEHOLD THE CHRIST:

I be hold the Christine you Today I would like to explored my though be had the Christ along with quotation ... One of the most difficult things we may have to do is allowing other to be different, Yet we can learn I to look past differences when we Len to look for and behold the christen every one: No matter how different others may seen to be, we remember that everyone was created by GOD, and their fore ever done is created good ...

We do not have to understand or ever approve of the actions of other In order to behold the Christine them. All we need is a willingness and a desire to bless others in our prayers.

Let us affirm: Behold the Christ in you. I give thanks for you and acknowledge that our difference are the very things that make us unique. I love and appear cheat you. I behold the Christ in you now and always,...I quote it ... Love the lord your God withal Your heart ... Love your neighbor as yourself, "---Mat how 22:37,39 I would like to touch into the Service of Dedication: The concluding act of action here which is never the less a single movement ... The prayers are presenting themselves unto -- all they value, all they possess -- yet machine into the LIFE of the world for responsible involvement.

Saturday, Nov 27/04, 11:54 pm more chapter My thought on patience: I am patient, for I know that God always answers my prayers. I relax and let go of concern about the "When" or "How" of answers to my prayers no matter how urgent my need seems to be (just like occurred me this last Fri. day between devil inspector of City and my workers I have to slow down if I listen to my angle daughter, but I am who I am he creates me for Who HEIS and he want for him so I got that done that day. His assistance in my patient and his as guard): Seems to be. I remember ed that most needs change but that God's help is constant.

I ask, believe, and act with the understanding that my prayers are being answered. The result is the kind of spiritual growth that I need for True peace and joy. My deepest desires are part of GOD's loving plan for me, and my faith lights the way to a better understanding of what that plan is. Placing my trust in the transforming power of faith, I do the best that I can at my daily tasks. Patiently, I wait for God's answers and enjoy the bountiful gifts of this day, "Thanks, God "thou dost keep him in perfect, whose mind is stayed on thee because he trusts in thee" - Isaiah 26:3 (the day two day after thanksgiving continue nov27/43:44 am):

WHERE is our hearts the since Christianity mean? My heart and mid are touched by the wisdom of God.... I take right action. Guidance: Am I experiencing the kind of problem that I don't do? I feel defeated even before I begin searching for an answer because the situation calls for more understanding, such the housing preparation situation of my property at NE occurred by city worker whom unethical mind and related it by my one of my work, etc., than I think I have ????

The answers to these questions and all other are coming, turn-ing to God in prayer so that my heart and my mind are aligned with divine intelligence, ... As a beloved child of GOD, I am heir to divine light. I open my mind and my heart to divine light, I grow in awareness of what is right for me ... God is the source of knowledge, and divine understanding is available tome when never I need it. When I rely on GOD's light and love, my eyes are open to TRUTH and my thinking becomes clear. With God's help, I take right action.

II Harmony:

After my spiritual angle daughter told me, papa, how's about making Than giving day to be a miracle: here is my mind is Harmony ... it is not my angel daughter's world but mush from h-HIM Via, my angel daughter.

So, I am willing to be harmonious, loving person in all my relationships... Weather are following a blueprint of a house of dishes, we know that the right materials or ingredients are essential for a successful outcome. This is why in order to live, work, or be in harmony with other to live, work, or be in harmony with other's we need to include all the right ingredients in our relationships with them ...

The good news is that GOD has already supplies us with the ingredients we need for harmonious, loving relationship...

We start with heaping measure of love, give for the joy of loving, not for something in return. We included generous portion of FAITH Fait in GOD working through us. We add a pinch of patience to allow the very best resort to come about.

Wes tire in apperception also ---for the spirit of GOD that is within each person at all times. I quoted, "For he is our peace, who has made us both one" Ephesians 2:14 (I am willing to continue more to very faith and harmony later one where it is a suitable chapter): (after thanksgiving 26/04) This is must be changed to be after the end of worship chapter:

We are American people, celebrated our survival from being death from hungry, from Native Indian people thought the hit how to eat and live and survive... now everyone celebrated that, included the writer my self. Can w things of the restore the world whom hungry has no refrigerator, no food no money to buy anything to feed themselves or their families? We ate here one mill equips to one week r a month for the rest of the world eat such the poorest of the poor people thinks in Thailand or India ... it is so as home for us can not think in the piratical reality of the sharing human being on earth. I feels we are, as America is, super Sal fished one on earth. We are hunting for imperialism capitalism for super world power but care only them salve care less nor are a tall for the rest of the world. I am so super dis-appointed this is why every thanksgiving day, every enjoyed so much at diner table but not me, how many billions of turkey were killing for day just human desirable and enjoyed, can you think of stopping killing Turkey they are our animals friends, and they wanted to live their lives as much as us..look at the world Hunger Belt and Empires of History. Let examined how many people who hungers in the world. In studying the major history, I have discovered an amazing fact --- the power belt historically of the notions lies in the middle of the world.

Look at the drawing in Appended C and readers will see what I meant. (I will write more on this later day) (November 25/04 at 1:25 am Thanksgiving day) I would like to ask you back to earlier thought of most popular in epilogs sophia thought that being influenced by Christianity Worshipers; Worshipers in the Christianity in the deepest sense them it, is abstract idea ... and those idle for those whom wanted or filling to be free from suffering and therefore, Worshipers need God, and God only the depend up on ... I will stated that those idle influenced by Leibniz or Descartes whom though the worshiper son substance where they divined the substance into Monads, numerology & plurality... for worshiper then each has different of individual substance which I would like described as it is predicated ... to some extends then to me when worshiper has an individual substance may be alike and differ only number all it, I mean they're the difference share understood in figured. For example, the substance of which all empirical things are composed, and I will used the idea of where called by Leibniz Monads." Worshipers then carried such ideas from their corporal things, which having certain character theistic where known plurality. And quality extension, motivation (movability), flexibility...Worshipers have not realizing that substance INDEPENDENCE in respect to creation, or any substance being only through creation and commences through annihilation, diminishes, through natural mean..., and those mean, although they frequently transformed in to numbers of substance neither augment nor diminishes. I will call edit its INTERNAL NATURE For worshipers get into the essence (inter nature) of substance For worship seeks for International of substance they need to conceive it by mind, and the in must be purified and free from those though, out of among creation substance. Tome then, as my mind clearly thought to share with readers here Between God and Creation of sub-stance,,, the creation of substance is like an entire world and likes a mirror of GOD ...Worshiper has struggling the cause of an idea, and it just as much reality (substance) as the idea represents ... the final cause and efficient cause proposition here then, the worships go couch of an idea, and it must as much reality (substance) as the idea represents ... the final cause and efficient cause proposition here then the worshipers got cauch of relationship among the type of sub stances, namely mentality and different kinds of substances which extend worshipers mind to have a relationship to GOD(ethical or causality) ... the Distinction here then the worshiper think that God produces different substances according to different views since God produces different substances according to different views since God has the world or his creation which I called the International of GOD, the appropriate nature of each substance corresponds what happening to all other without, however, their acting upon one another directly.

I would like to etherize and the problems of worshipers of all of their point I feel the base on the rival I system, and that lets to skepticism (which I will later one emphasized with the idea of Hume though and my VIA Buddhist influenced us ... in the last or very vary chapter so reads must keep it in mind) The reason BEING I will conclude that there are external material things, mater cons stinting of primary qualities, which has an extended, destine and independent on of their being perceived ...What is perception to Worships? Those are everything we perceived cannot exist otherwise than in worshipers' minds where they perceive them, what we perceive besides our own ideals and sensations ... further Moe, what rely problem worshipers have that the idea of perception and believe in it so since they believe in it which it is impossible for worshipers to have knowledge of this mater distance from perception or the MIND, why? Because all perception has its FOUNDATION in the mind ... I know that the worshippers think of nothing more than an idea of their own mind and, therefore, cannot exist outside perception. Here, the real problem of worshiper then they cannot miss perception if they reflect on what passes within their one mind, and the idea of sensation of material matter are nothing more then that what has passed within their minds:

Note: My lecture for winter quarter 1972, (therefore should consulting more these concept of idea to my note in same quarter next page winter 1972.

Next session, I would add hereto the world and its sufferings of mind find and that where worshipers need safer and has notion of pending and that pending is upon GOD only see my lecture in the same quaver) Green book):

I could like emphasized the worshipers ACT of deviation in the presentation of the offering. Here, these worshipers again offering up themselves in offering UNTOGOD their worldly possession. It is an offering that is made, not a collection which taken ... one must aware of that what is given is but a token in diction that all of our goods are gifts to be used in responsible living in the world.

At the close of the procession, a prayers of dedication is made, signifying this action is intended for GOD's glory and service of the neighbor. At This time and this point, the players break forth into a doxology or hymn of praise to GOD the Father, Son, and Holy Spirit, which is a fitting finale to ACT Two and the whole realm of salvation. Act Three is a drama at enactment of life in the Holy Spirit --- It is a life of utter dependence upon GOD and utter responsibility for the world, gift to all who rejoice in the Lord through the forgiveness of their sins.

After the epilogue, which may consist of hymn which once again indicates and honors the COD we stand before, plus a benediction, the actors leave the repentance, thankful praise, and creative love.

One day --- tomorrow perhaps, they will return to rehearse ah-gain the drama of their Sal ration that they may remember new who and hose they ARE> The end of this chapter).

(November 24/04, the day before Thanksgiving day ... must be continues from 24/ of this day morning):

I would like to further pointed out for my brother and sisters who read this session to be realized that the worshipers are here offering up themselves to CDO by placing in HIS hands and offering up themselves in presenting to COD their responsibility in and for the world.

In Brief then, the Prayers, having received themselves and the world as CIFTS from GO, are offering them back again.

Let us be precisely awarded that Prayers are made for the church and then for the home and the state, the (finally) economic life. It includes the educational institutions and the international structures...

The worshipers then turn with particular concern for those living at far edge of being forced out of these natural order.

Intersession are now offered for the poor and hungry (it easy and so obviously to see many priest referred to these): the sick and those in person for the outcasts and those who have lost the kindly light of reason and those who are on beds of death, in this action the community boldly involving itself in life as and daringly entering into the existence of other CREATIONS:

Further, I would like to pointed it out again: The first scene beginnings with maces of petition and supplication. The prayers are not engaged in manipulation of cosmic power, but rather they are surrendering into GOD's hands their future and destiny the worshippers have tuned their daily care over to the one wise, forgiving presence is everywhere and precisely here in the DARKNESS of the UNKNOWN.

December 02/04 at 5:52 am in the morning: This chapter: INNER PEACE

After I have real legal total with unethical business associated partner whom I have conducted business over ten years, I am so frication with this word that insulting my wife and my English pronunciation and his limed that the is doing notion wrong from what his people did ... to us cause my trip short and in urgent from Thailand to come and continue business relationship with him and his people was unreliable to do anymore work broken promised my plumb ling did not do anything wrong either intern of helping my tenants begin thigh order to use so what is law and is illegal lawful to me is making nosense ... If I have no peace of mud or Inner Peace I should continue to fight and stated that my people did not a anything wrong as long as sati factory my tenants and me and that was count for then my enemy friend has no judge it is most frustrating and disturbing so much o deal with dishonored business company and do nodular many mistake and claim he nor his people did not do anything wrong by trying tar-bush off, big timer ... whatever he said only what it mean it les ... well enough for enough.

My heart told me, so my mind are touché the of god. I am peaceful and secure, I radiance to the world when I am at peace in my mind and heart. I begin to feel at peace when I allow to ask in and through me when I allow divine love to fill me with peace.

Inner peace is not something that can be forced. I experience inner peace only when I relax and let GOD's love fill me through and through. Touched by the love of GOD, I know that god and I are one that all is well in my world... I can maintain this scans of peace and well-being regardless of or events. When Chaos appears, when situations seem to speak of anything but peace, I FOCUS my the potential for peace in every situation. I bless all involved and know that God's Love and Order work to bless and promote spiritual growth. "peace I leave with you: my peace 1 give to", --John 14:27.

December 02/04 Faith

I got a call from one of my contractor company said there was a bad news. As in silence, I said what program? What else bad news I am going to here. He said inspector came over and said we need to pulled permission of all work, and he said that, do not worry. Everything must be fine. Please meet him next or so. I am confuse why? What? I am only doing good karma, what? And why? Bad karma return back to me. Well, let's call me and have faith in HIM, my hearts, myself...

My Strong faith in God keeps me concentrate and do right action.

Fear can render us incapable of creative thinking or ring action only if we let it --- instead of reacting with fear when we hear disturbing news. Let us meet such news with instant, steadfast FAITH:

The Power of God is mighty to adjust, harmonize, head I, and inspire.. our stand fast faith in god accuses us to turn from fearful thoughts to a deep respect for the power of God at work to bring forth good. We give thanks that good judgment and right action prevail at all fortifies us. We become more optimistic because we know that God is good, and good is the only power there is --- we are centered and ready to take the right action at right time, our strong faith always us through.

"I fear no evil; for thou are with me" ---Psalm 23:4

December 03/04:

Protection

There is nothing greater than the protection of God.

The presence of god is active in my life, and I am protected.

No matter where I am, I knowledge that God's presence is continually with me. God and I are one and cannot be separated. Whether I am traveling to new places or staying in the comfort of own home, I know that I am never alone.

My family and friends are never alone either ... I release any anxieties about their well-being, for I know that, too, are being divinely protect throughout the day and niter.

Through prayer and my belief that all is well, I free my mind from anxiety or concern, and my way is clear to enjoy the day ...The presence of god is active I, and my life are in the lives of my loved ones. --- We are protected.

"Every word of GOD proves he is a shields to those who take refuge in him", --- Proverbs 30:5.

HEALING

I have the most hard time in my life. My mother is passed away, my sister I disowned, my pre-daughter-in-law excommunicate time ... I didn't see my three grandchildren, I have a huge problem with contractors in my business whom this not listen to my ordered financially, accuse me big loss, and I lost my face as being reliable Thailand men forth and so on continually ... I know that there are a lot of people whom may have more problems and suffering than me, but now my family business mission trip has postponed everything has to cause me unhearing from the death of my family, death after death, my brother died a few year ago, and again my younger brother died and my mother recently died, how do I can cope with this serious human suffering and human depression:

This chapter, why I am writing on healing, it will help my readers as well as help me: Perhaps at the time I need healing the most, I feel that I lack the strength, faith, or understanding to be healed.

I put aside all doubt and know that it is the life of God that heals me ... I remember that Jesus prayed before he healed one person or a whole crowd, so do I, I pray, realizing that prayer is an important part of my life or my healing process.

APPENDIX PART ONE

Special memory of Dorothy Balch, my lovely mother-in-law (November 29, 2009)

Pastor, family, friends, and all special guests,

Today is the beginning after the journey of Dorothy's life ended. God, the author of her life, closed the chapter of her lifetime, and He will lead or write a new chapter of her other life in Heaven. God is the only one who determines her life just as He does for all of us. There is no question about this subject.

Let me introduce myself. I am Daney Dumdeang, one of her sons-in-law. I am so proud and honored to be member of the Balch family. I am sure there is nothing new in human life. All of us have experienced about the sorrow which make us unhappy miserable. In fact, the story of Dorothy's life showing here in this church is not really like what she has already done all along her lifetime. We could write and talk about it more than thousands of pages and never end. There is too much to say or to do in our life time but today's event is dedicated to the life of Dorothy, my mother-in-law. So, we will take this moment to share what we can do for her.

My dearest friend, a pastor from India wrote to me: *"I saw the memorial service invitation and the message printed in, it is just like an invitation given by the heavenly Father himself. Mother Dorothy, indeed, she is a great soul, most loved one to our Lord and Savior..."*

Jesus Christ, only words are not sufficient to describe her human quality, her faith and her love and incomparable care for everyone. I lift up my two hands in praise to thank to the Lord for giving such a beautiful person to become a great blessing to a big family on earth and for keeping her safe until we will meet her again one day.

My mother-in-law, Dorothy, is a great and noble person. She has conducted her four noble paths. Her actions were considered good deeds or Karma, which she has performed for us all her life. No doubt that she should be in Heaven now. We know and accept that God is the only author of our lives. He set our life path since the first chapter and continue to the end, the last chapter. Now, He has closed His chapter about Dorothy's life. He has done His work for her in this life and He would continue to do for her in another life ... in Heaven. So, the work of God has no ending and no beginning.

We then looked at the world and may found that it was good to ask such a question because even life is sin, the people in the West may agree on maybe not. Anyway, they affirmed that the question was worth asking. To explains this idea, let me begin with the story of myself. I am a former Theravada Buddhist monks, I truly believe that that kind of question is valid and confirms the point of the first noble truths, and it is also a reputation service of Christian God. Look how miserable life is, and it is hard to accept the God's verdict on His work. But why don't we look the other side of life, such as "let go of things related to our body, emotions, and feelings and gain our glimpse of deathlessness or immortality of what is like to be totally free from suffering." To do so, we should understand and can identify our suffering or pain of our life in this material world, and then we can be free and let it go, and we will attain to release our pain. It will help us little by little to go higher and higher on the ladder until we find ourselves securely on the top. And we can finally go out of the ladder, and we will be totally free. We have to grow up and should not cling to anyone or anything. So we can clearly understand, suffering and end this suffering. This is my hope for everybody, hope that we all can sort out that which parts of our lives are truth and truth to what? Hope that one day in this life, we will find the brightness at the point. Oh, yes, it is the end of our suffering and to be totally free from everything.

For us and each of us, we should realize ourselves that in western culture, we believe that God is our refuge and our strength, our helper in each problems ... And today, we lost our beloved ones, my mother-in-law. Dorothy, we are in deep sorrow. But we have to realize that death is like sleeping. Living is like dreaming between death and life in the hereafter. The physical body is dead, but the conscious mind may remain because the internal separation has not yet happened. To me, as a former Buddhist practitioner, I truly believe that life is "anicca" or impermanent and constantly changing, such birth and death. There is no permanent substance in human body or "anatta". Life is in itself. If the human body is destroyed, the spirituality has never been destroyed. It permanently remains in the universe. This is what I want to say about my beloved mother-in-law, who is a tough lady and has been fighting for her life for a while. She was so direct to what she wanted. One of her medical doctors told us that my mother-in-law was a very tough lady. She has fought for her life. So all, her medical team said that at her situation, the doctors can do nothing. They could only just comfort her and heal her from pain.

My lovely mother-in-law taught me that life is beautiful, life is love, life is immortal. One of my sons told us that his Grandma was full of love, so let her love be fulfilled by our love. She would feel our love and would wake up and return home with us. She would be O.K.

I think that my son can't accept death yet. Death is only another process or step of life; therefore, death is nothing, and it is zero. My mother-in-law loved everyone whom I love, such as some of my cousins; Nirun and his family, Chin and his family, Sue Jin and Maddy, Marion and her family, Michele and other. She loved all of them and treated them like her family members, even our pets, she loves all of them the same way as us too. Mom is really special and unique. Her love is above and beyond human characteristics. This is why my sister, Linda, and my wife agreed to engrave these words on her name plaque: "Beloved, beloved, beloved." I know that Mom will tell us something like in this poem, while we are weeping, morning and crying ... showing our emotional love to her.

On Wednesday night, she has awaken and asked if she still alive. *"Yes, you are alive,"* we answered. It seems that some of us laughed at her question. So she continued asking, *"I say something wrong?"* We all answered, *"No, you said nothing wrong."* Later, she told me while I meditated that she was in heaven with all the rest of our family. She returned to this world and felt differently to see all of us surrounding her in the hospital patient room. So, she questioned if she was alive in the sense of human life. But at that time, I know that He has already taken her life in heaven. That is why she remain asking the same question, *"Am I alive?"* And that, she was in her mystical time and gave her final words to all of us. I believe that life after death exist and it is real.

Now, I will conclude my testimony for my beloved mother-in-law. We all have life because we are here, and we are here because we have life. We are together here in the place that is like a resting place from our long Lenten journey of Faith. May everyone continue walking from here with a new spirit and with your heads set straight and high. I am sure that you all exactly agree with me that it is uncertain where this week will take us to, but the only certain thing is that we will never travel alone. Thanks to God.

Farewell, farewell, farewell, my lovely mother-in-law, Dorothy...

We will meet and be together again soon.

Thank you, everybody, wholeheartedly for your kind consideration to be here today, to honor and to celebrate a new life of Dorothy Balch. She certainly knows what we have done for her, as she loves all of us ... she is here with us as well.

God bless you all, Daney Dumdeang.

Your beloved and faithful son-in-laws

APPENDIX PART TWO

May 23rd, 2005

The author negotiated with Red Cross-World Vision on helping the Sri Lanka Tsunami Victims to rebuild the houses, schools, hospital, churches, Buddhist Temples, and the Mosque in Ambalangoda.

These two pictures on the left are the capitol Hill Church, where Patty and I invited my assistant, Tom, to give a speech on Nong Thian Thip.

The Capitol Hill Church have been built and continued active for more than a hundred years … Now, it is no longer in service due to lack of funds to maintain the building and to pay for earthquake and fire insurance.

Old members have gone to heaven, no young generation continue.. the church left only the good memory in our heart. My family and my wife's family have attended this church over 50 years … So I am proud to show the significant and unforgettable picture in my book and also on the back cover of it too.

Thanks

Patty and I have totally committed ourselves to religious and spiritual aspects to guide our lives. This year, both of us have done our vow of marriage to refresh our closeness and spirituality to the higher level of our lives. We both are happier that we get more time together this year than we have ever had before. We are learning more about each other and understanding each other more and more.

I believe all of us shoot to do the same in order to live happily and peacefully together in the world, in the family, in the community, society, and country where we live.

God bless all of you, and may God be with you.

SPECIAL FAREWELL TESTIMONY FOR PASTOR CHO OF THE CAPITOL HILL CHURCH

My Brothers, sisters, Young people, Pastor Cho and his family and all Pastors,

Honestly, it is not easy for me to write this farewell message as my purpose of writing is to express our deep gratitude and appreciation to Pastor Cho. I feel that it is significant of having been privileged to do so. It is such a great honor to me to be a long-lasting member of the Capitol Hill Church, to know all of you as we are God's family and share together our good news or bad news every Sunday, to know many pastors of the church both in the past and in the present, to have a great music director of the church, to have a special choir, to have a biggest smile from our SR Pastor who open the door and welcome us every Sunday, to have a great young Ministry, to have a friendly social coffee hour; chatting cheerfully with one another, sharing our growing spirits and struggling with ourselves to find common ground which is a fundamental foundations of a Christion faith to seek the unity of Faith in God.

"We search and search until we all reach unity in the Faith and in the knowledge of the Son of God." (Ephesian 4:12-13) We gather together and we receive what really the word of God is. We give love to one another. We love everyone in the church as our family member. We share our love in our community. We share our love with everybody in the nation and with people of other nations, too. So the Capitol Hill Church is one of the most special and unique church in the history of our time and all the time of our next generations as well. Because all of us do it and have made it. We care for one another, and because of doing that, we develop our spiritual mind in that work. And that is the work that all of us has done, showing our love and our concern to many nations: Thailand, India, Korea, Jamaica, and around the world. And this will tell a lot about ourselves who we are,

as written in the Capitol Hill United Methodist Church: *"The mission of Capitol Hill Church is to be a caring congregation with God and the teaching of Jesus Christ, to serve the Church, the surrounding community, and the world ..."* And that is what we all are. We should be proud of ourselves. Moreover, we will comfort each other when one of us loses a family-loving member. And we will feel closer and closer to one another because that is the Way of God. One may not realize it. But that is what we are as members of Capitol Hill Church.

This story reminded me of the memory of one Sunday many years ago. When I had a Godly conversation with Howard Pinkstaff and Duane Johnson during our coffee hour.

Duane told me, *"Sit down with us, Daney. Why are you so quiet?"* I answered, *"He was silent for me and you. Why are we not silent, too."*

Duane continued asking, *"What the hell? Who are you? Anyway, are you Buddhist or Christian?"*

I looked at Howard and asked him, *"Who am I, Howard? Do you know?"*

Howard said, *"Hell, I don't know. I don't even know who I am either, Daney."*

I said, *"Who cares as long as we know we are God's creation. I think you and I are His creation, too, Duane. That is my answer from Him."*

The three of us were in a silent moment like we were in the state of a short meditation, and then Howard said, *"We feel like we are crying now, Daney"* I said, *"Yes, I am."*

Howard said, *"But I don't see your tears."*

I said, *"My tears are inside my heart, and now I am in the midst of my tears. That's why I am in silence. We all are".*

Howard said, *"Right, I bet you're damn right, Daney. I think you are really a Christian believer more than us, Daney. And you have two foundations of Faith."*

I said, *"Yes, you got me! All my life, I feel and believe that the way the Lord represents the way he got the enlightenment is the same as Jesus Christ represents the way to the Father."*

Duane said, *"Right on, Daney, we can buy that."*

I replied, *"Thanks!"*

Duane said, *"Thanks for sitting with us."*

I replied, *"You are welcome."*

I told Duane and Howard that being Christian is the vocation to which we have been called by God ... this is my realization. *"That's very heavy and very true, Daney."* We continue to encounter with God and ask Him to enter our lives, and then let Him take control of our lives. We do not make a request, we should stay still and turn ourselves to Him. "What words should I give you, guys" I told Duane and Howard.

Since that day, I have been able to realize our precious gift of conversation and I have taken it as the gift of absolute Faith in God. From that day until now, no matter how bad things have been happened in my life, I have never doubted anymore the ever-present of God. God made me learn how to love myself and love others. I would love others and want to be loved by others. I can tell you that he or she or neither may encounter with God; as a personal encounters loving God, experiencing God in a way that one can feel, or as a personal being or truth, which is neither being nor non-being. It is a unity, which has many, many manifestations in many religions, including Buddhism. We credit God with the creator of the universe. We are in the same nation, with the same God. God is only over Hope, and His hope is our Hope, too. It seems that real faith in Christianity has been broken, and we have to restore it. God wants us to restore His love to one another, as He has His love to His father, and to us. So, we should give love as God gives His love to us. And His love is ultimate, supreme love, not a false or fake love which involved in sexual feeling or artificial love. And it is meaningless from an ultimate love. Love of God can save our marriage life, and the divorce percentage may reduce or go down to zero, and the married life in the USA will last forever. Then, our children will no longer be alone and feel lonely. Families life in The USA will be stable as others outside the USA expect for us. Psychologists, like our Dr. Phil will be out of job. Therefore, we must practice the Love of God and again, please remember, the Love of God alone will save our World. The war will end, and we will arrive to human utopia, which is eternal peace, which is God's will that is written to us as happiness. All of this is our eternal heritage from Him, or we may say Niravana.

Thank you, my dear friends, Douane and Howard, for the best godly conversation we have had together. Both of you will always be in my heart forever. I will never, never forget our special time we have been together.

Now, let's return to my story. What has turned me to continue a journey into the heart of God?

"I fled Him down the nights and the days. I fled Him down the arches of the years.

I fled Him down the labyrinthine ways of my own mind and in the midst of tears.

I hid away from Him!"

These are the best words I can relate to. It is one of the poems from The Hound of Heaven by a victory poet, Francis Thompson. Do you know it is the way to find God? Did God make a mistake in creating me and you to be one of His children or His family. I don't think so, as He has never separated us from one another, but He has given us His unity. He loves all of us no matter who we are or what kind of gender we are, as long as we are his creation. And this is what I realized by myself, and it is that the way He gave to me and to share with all of you today.

In addition, I feel deeply and especially to be blessed to have my special person in my life who is a real Christian believer. Since the first day I have met her, she looks graceful with her Christian Faith. Deva, or God's messenger, introduced me to her while I was in the flight back to Thailand after conducting the Buddhism conference in Burma. God led me to meet her in His image and His vision, and He led her to meet me, too. Guess who is that mythical lady who has a beautiful heart and full of Christian love and faith in her mind? Yes, that person is my wife, whom I married and live with to this day.

I was born and raised in the Eastern World. When I grew up, I practiced the doctrine of Buddhist Theravada, but God led me meet my soulmate. It is a mythical story above and beyond my knowledge to explain. It is God's way, not my way. Anyway Thanks to Him for making us to be His children. One day, on the way to the play, and I was with Allen, he asked me how my wife and I met. I told him, *"My angel made me see her as a mythical vision before I met her and told me that she is my soulmate."* And I asked him back how he met his wife. Allen said, *"Oh no, your story is better than mine."*

He made me laugh, and we all laughed together. It seems to be a joke laughing matter, but I could not deny my experience about the existence of God, being with Him, and how He has worked for my life, or how He has blessed me, changed me, encouraged me, or even broke me and healed me. I got beyond the realm of knowledge to the realm of relationship with God. I am certain about this, and I am sure that once in your lifetime, all of you will have the experience with God like I did and without doubt. And this is what I sincerely want to tell you so you can see it clearly what God has done for me. Thank God, He leads me to my wife, who is the strongest

Christian believer. As her brother has already said that, I am very lucky to have a real Christian, firm faith in God as my wife. Yes, I am. Thank God, I would like to thank Him again for giving me three children, four grandchildren, and many adopted god-children in Thailand and around the world.

Some of them are with me today. Thanks God for making me to meet all of you. I will never be able to thank God enough throughout my life for making me know each of you. That is the way that I've always thought about. To understand ourselves and to love ourselves is to understand God and to love god. To return to His love is to accept sincerely His commitment, follow him every steps, and doing what His words say. (John 36:32)

Even though we are sinners, but we are still loved by God, as He created all of us. We are His creation. So logically and ultimately, we are part of Him, and He is part of us. We cannot deny this. Prayer of St. Francis of Assisi says, *"Lord, make me an instrument of your peace, where there is hatred, let me see love; when there is injury, pardon; where there is doubt, fact; where there is despair, hope; where there is darkness, light, where there is sadness, joy.*

Today is a special day because it is Mother's Day. Happy Mothers' Day to all of mothers in the world, including Mather Mary. The word "mother" in the Sanskrit language comes from "mata," which means "permanent and eternal love." that's the love of mothers which love their children unconditionally and forever. Without woman or mother, there wouldn't have Jesus Christ or Lord or no man on earth. So, in such a special spiritual day, it was a great honor for me to deliver this speech today. What else do I need, or do we need? Nothing else is needed for as we have a growing spirit for this church. But to share my real feeling with all of you here today, I have to honestly say that I was shocked when I learned that Pastor Cho is leaving the Capitol Hill Church. It's unexpected and too fast. Truly, I feel both sad and happy at the same time. My feeling is mixed up, and it is not so easy for me to say goodbye. I have never written any fare-well message to the previous pastors, but I have been told in His silent voice to do it after my wife informed me that Pastor Cho was going to leave our church by

June this year. Honestly and sincerely to do this is not really my intention on behalf of me alone, but I do it on behalf of all of us, all of the church members as well. And I need a lot of prayers to encourage myself to accept the command of Him in doing this special testimony.

So please be patient and bear up well with me. Open your hearts, your ears, your minds to listen to the special message that is from Him rather than from me or from all of you.

First of all, I would like to express my appreciation to the Church Authority Committee, who welcomed and chose Pastor Cho for this church. Up until now, Pastor Cho has been with us for over 4 years. It is the best choice and excellent work of the committee to choose Pastor Cho to be here. However, as I am not part of the decision committee, but my wife is, so I couldn't have been more disappointed than this. You know, in Thailand, where I came from, when a senior monk is appointed to be an abbot of any temple, he will remain in that position until the day he dies. But, the system of Christian church in the United States of America is different. There is a hierarchical pastoral system. It seems to me that the Christian Religion here is managed like an aspects of politics. It upset me, and I think that it may upset some of you as well. Because of the method that pastors have to move around after they know very well their ministry, their people and their community. What I say here I don't blame the Christian people or all of you in this church, but the power of management system is more political than pure religious practice. However, throughout the past several decades, there are many pastors who came to work at this church, some are good in the eyes of the administrators but not in the eyes of God.

Pastor Cho is a brilliant, hard-working, kind, warm to be with him. He has a good heart. After all, he is always in a good mood and has a sense of humor. Each time he gives a sermon to us, he can find the way to make us laugh. We will miss you, Pastor Cho and your family too. I want to cry and so disappointed. I cannot shed my tears. Being a man, I have to control myself, but ... *"He will wipe every tear from their eyes. There will be no more death or mourning, or crying or pain, for the old order of things has passed away."* (Revelation 21:4) We, as the Capitol Hill Church members, have the common ground. We are growing in moral and spiritual power because we have faith in Him. That means we must realize that we must go above and beyond the socio-cultural and biological norm (male or female gender). We have to focus on the word of God, which is full of love and it is a holy word, no matter who it is taught or where it is heard. We should not be obsessed with the biological or socio-cultural consensus on the subject of gender. Such an opinion has been accepted for a long time in the history, and recently, it has been challenged by new ideas. But first and foremost thing of true Christian is that they must uphold God's sovereignty in which one part is the death of Jesus Christ as He died for all of us, not for any single gender (Ps 83:18). And as it was pointed out in our first meeting with our new pastor on Sunday, April 19, 20, 2010 that we must focus on teaching the word of God, I would like to encourage everybody here that there is only one time which is essential time to do that. And that time is Now.

To conclude, as we all recognize that to live our lives is not easy as it is full of pain, sin, sorrow, but Jesus has removed our sins with His death. By the way, Lord has shown the way of freedom by following his doctrine; the Four Noble Truths. Of course, life is also joyful and happy as long as we follow His way, *"I am the way, the truth, and the life. No one can come to the Father except through me"* (John 14:6). *"You make known to me the path of life; you will fill me with joy in your presence ..."* (Psalm 16:11)

There is a poem:

> May we all renew and restore our fundamental Christian faith on the principle of commitment and unify our love with God's love. His love is the highest principle; no hatred, never divided black or white, male or female, guy or lesbian or transgender as he has given it to all human beings. What we need in our Christian church, in our community, in the United States of America, and in the rest of the world is no separation, no violence, no discrimination, no lawlessness, but love on the Noble path of wisdom and the

compassion of God. Let us, as strong Christian, dedicate ourselves to what Ancient Greek tragedian Aeschylus wrote, "Tame the savageness of man and make gentle the life of this world," and everyone would better know that the Capitol Hill Church is always opened the door for him and his family.

So, Lord, we lift up our hands to Pastor Cho, his wife, his children, and all his family, please place Pastor Cho in the highest shelter to rest in the shadow of God Almighty.

We will say of the Lord, you are their refuge and fortress, you will preserve their family time. You will cover their home; you will command your angels to protect them as they travel. You will help them win the lost. You have said, *"I will be with (them), with a long life, I will deliver (them) and show (them) my salvation."* In the name of Jesus, we, all members of the Capitol Hill Church, cancel all assignments to do to the enemy who is against them.

Farewell, farewell, farewell Pastor Cho and his family, and welcome David Weekly and his family to the Capitol Hill Church, and the ultimately welcome to the Heavenly Father to our heart.

Goodbyes are not forever; Goodbyes are not the end. They simply mean we miss you until we meet again ... May God be with you, and You are in Him.

Daney Dumdeang

On behalf of the Capitol Hill Church

NOTE ON THE FAREWELL TESTIMONY TO PASTOR CHO ON SUNDAY, MAY 9/2010

Following are the opinions of some people on the author's Farewell Speech for Pastor Cho:

There have been many more people who have told me that the speech I gave was very good. But I apologize for not being able to put it all into this note.

Some Anecdotes about Pastor Cho

Story 1

I am just a little Thai-American man in this church. I am not a significant person and don't have enough weight to say anything. I only have faith. And my faith is so strong and real to Him. And that is how I do know myself.

"Even if I testify on my own behalf, my testimony is valid for I know where I came from and where I am going, but you have no idea when I come from or where I am going to." (John 8:14) *"You judge according to flesh; I judge no one!"* (John 8:15) Well, this letter is not about all. It's all about me. Just wanted to let you know and to share my awareness of what bothered me about the Christian hierarchy, which has increased year after year. While I sincerely commit myself to Jesus and congregation of the church, as a Christian believer, I found the increasing of Christianity involving in politics and politicians. It looks like a corruption of Christian administration. To me, this involvement does not bring us anything in return for our spiritual life. We must pursue our own spiritual quest independently without any dogmatic authoritarianism and doctrines. We must focus on the moral values rather than the political and social issues. If you are raising the

question, are you really speaking for God, and is God talking through you as His instruments? Clearly, I have to admit that the corruption in the Christian mind in the USA and in the rest of the world, including my country, Thailand, is the enemy of God. *"Yet even if I do judge my decisions are true, because I am not alone, I stand with the Father, who sent me!"* (John 8:16-18) I don't know what all of you think. But this is what I am thinking.

We, as Christian, we are caught up in materialism without knowing who we are; we use the symbolism of spirit mind rather than really, really aware of the true meaning of spiritual relationship of Christianity. I am not against having nice and beautiful things but the extravagance is not the will of God. Our treasure should be in heaven, and our earthly goods should be based on the mindset of what will be left behind when we leave. The most central focus of real Christian must not be a negative reflection on the Christian faith, which will minimize the charitable giving by the people. What saddened me is that many people who donate to charity organizations or Ministries think that they will have a lavish lifestyle as a result of their donation to charity.

My message to you is about some point of my life, I have grown out of that kind of donation, giving up my house, my time, my life, and my everything to the poor in India, but finally, I found that it is not my holy or spiritual life. I have not yet reach the peak of my spiritual life as Jesus wants for me. I can do nothing as I am just a radical Christian, and I was a former scholar and Buddhist monk, and now I am a Christian believer. I left the Christian politics out of my life and dealt with what I was being called and order to do by Him. He has made me realize that my spiritual practice that, most often associated with Buddhism, have a place in the life of Christian and that I can tell you that the more I listened to Pastor Cho, the more I realized that I have a strong Faith. Pastor Cho has shown me and all of us that God is the Source of Faith. This does not imply that we have to increase our faith in Him. But my Faith grows because God has the qualities that induce us to trust in Him.

Over 12 years ago, my secretary, whom I trusted and loved as my god-daughter, edited my manuscript, told me, and encouraged me to continue my teaching on Faith. She seriously told me, *"Papa, I really read what you have written on worship. You clearly expressed your real Faith in God. I highly respect it. It makes me feel close to Him. Please, Papa, keep writing and put your thoughts down in writing. They will be going somewhere ... your thought of Faith can spiritually help people."* Thank God, she truly inspired me. I am not an extraordinary man like Pastor Cho or Billy Graham, who was born in the Christian Faith, but I am able to express my thoughts that came from Him. And it is Him alone who guides me to my own being.

My decisions are true because I am not alone. I stand with the Father, who sent me! (John 8:16-18) I don't know what all of You think. But this is what I am thinking.

We, as Christian, we are caught up in materialism without knowing who we are; we use the symbolism of spirit mind rather than really, really aware of the true meaning of spiritual relationship of Christianity. I am not against having nice and beautiful things but the extravagance is not the will of God. Our treasure should be in heaven, and our earthly goods should be based on the mindset of what will be left behind when we leave. The most central focus of real Christians must not be a negative reflection on the Christian faith, which will minimize the charitable giving by the people. What saddened me is that many people who donate to Christian Organizations or the ministry think that they will have a lavish lifestyle as a result of their donation to charity.

My message to you is about some point of my life, I have grown out of that kind of donation, giving up my house, my time, my life, and my everything to the poor in India, but finally, I found that it is not my holy or spiritual life. I have not yet reach the peak of my spiritual life as Jesus wants for me. I can do nothing. I am just a radical Christian, as I was a former. Scholar and Buddhist monk and now I am a Christian believer. I left the Christian politics out of my life and dealt with what I was being called and order to do by Him. He has made me realize that my spiritual practice, most often associated with Buddhism, have a place in the life of Christian and that I can tell you that the more I listened to Pastor Cho, the more I realize that I have a strong Faith. Pastor Cho has shown me and all of us that God is the Source of Faith. This does not imply that we have to increase our faith in Him. But my Faith grows because God has the qualities that induce us to trust in Him.

Over 12 years ago, my secretary, whom I trusted and loved as my god-daughter has, edited my manuscript, told me and encouraged me to continue my teaching on Faith. She seriously told me, *"Papa, I really read what you have written on worship. You clearly expressed your real Faith in God. I highly respect it, It makes me feel close to Him. Please, Papa, keep writing and put your thought down in writing. They will be going somewhere ... and they, your thought of Faith, can spiritually help people."* Thank God, she truly inspired me. I am not an extraordinary man like Pastor Cho or Billy Graham, who are born in the Christian faith, but I am able to express my thought that came from Him. And it is Him alone who guides me to my own being.

Story 2

Pastor Cho was sent from the East for the spiritual and pilgrimage mission for the West. Undoubtedly, he is a hard-working young man for God's ministry because of his sincerity and honesty on his work. He has gone above and beyond what we are expecting him to do. He is everything. Again, I will say that I do know, and I am sure all of you, too, that we have already increased our spiritual growth and strengthened our Faith. *"Paul says; Follow my example, as I follow the example of Christ."* (1 Corinthians 11:1).

We all know that Jesus Christ is the ultimate example of what it truly mean to be Christian Spirituality. When I can think clearly like this, I learn that I have spiritual growth, and so do you. *"... and continues in it, not forgetting what they have heard, but doing it -he will be blessed in what they do."* (James1:23-25). God chooses what we will be. Pastor Cho guided me to realize and believe this. I am certain that he touches each of our hearts the same way as he does to me.

Story 3

I often tell myself that the questions we should not ask are: Do we have faith? Is our faith enough? Because such questions like that will drive us to the darkness and to feel desperate. We should raise the questions as: Is God trustworthy? Is God believable? Will God relinquish His promise? Are God's power and love real? And the more we asked question and try to find the answer, the less likely we are. We are to find Faith in God. I do realize this from Pastor Cho's sermon.

If we gather together and turn our attention to God, we will right away discover the faith that will be raised in us. We are not the source of our faith. So the more we look at the true faith in God, Himself ... and wait and meditate, the more faith we will have. My given Faith and yours will bring us to perceive spiritual life as I always perceive in His silent voice. *"Then he said to them all: whoever wants to be my disciple must deny themselves and take up their Cross daily and follow me."* (Luke 9:23)

Today, Pastor made me realize the word of god is vital than ever. To me and to each of us.

Story 4

After searching for a new church, the word of God has come to me, as He is speaking to me. *"Father, I want those you have given me and to be with me. When I am and to see my glory, the glory you have given me because you love me before the creation of the world."* (John 17:24)

In connection to this essential point, His words make me realize that Lord and Jesus Christ have the same real and vital messages to all of us and everyone, regardless of religion. The word of god can be delivered by male, female, or transgender, as long as His word has been assigned by Him. Moreover, it has never been found that His mission must be done only by male or female or nothing else.

As it is clear, I have to stop searching my new church. Because there are many churches that I choose, then I changed my mind. It is my choice, not God's choice. And I noticed that I would never find a perfect church for me. As I was asked, and open my heart to stay on the Capitol Hill Church with all of you. And maybe one day, we will find that the Capitol Hill Churches is a perfect one for me with the guiding of God and for all of us too.

Then I decided to stay. I remember on the very, very first Sunday, I met Cho in the congregation after giving his first sermon. I had a chance to introduce myself to him and personally welcome him in our church. I am impressed with him. I also encouraged him for his English language. Now, it seems that his English is far away better than mine. Thank God for helping him develop his English quickly. I hope that you all understand him better by listening to what I'm talking about.

Thanks Lord, for taking care of him, giving him the brilliant abilities to deal with your word. Cho, please take your ministry do your duty with all your heart and soul.

Story 5

I mentioned in my last testimony 6 months ago that Pastor Cho was called from the East to wake up us to reemphasize and to remind us what we have fundamentally lost. Pastor Cho is the spiritual man from the East who was assigned to serve the great ministry and God's mercy. Jesus has given him to us. *"Go ye into all the world and preach the good news to everyone."* (Mark 16:15). Preaching mission is what He is going to do as He has already done until on the cross. And so, it is up to see this one fulfilled. All the end of the earth shall remember and shall know, and all will come and worship for the Kingdom of the Lord. For this point, I would like to ask you all to join together. Jesus commands us to continue His mission. He calls us not only to come to Him but also to go for Him. The mission of Jesus is so essential. There are five practical ways we can continue His mission. He has repeated these different ways in five different books of the Bible. It is as if he really wants this. And if we study these five ways, we'll learn the details of our mission in this world.

When we my wife and I visited our dear friend, Sam, we listened to the CD of Pastor Jerry Porter together. Jerry mentioned that Jesus wants us to go, preach, and pray, blessing and sharing what is tough to all nation. I am sure that all of you will probably find out that in the 18th, 19th, and even in the 20th centuries, everybody will do a great mission. *"Therefore go and make disciples of all nations, baptizing them in the name of the Father and of the son and of the Holy Spirit. Teaching them to observe all things whatsoever I have commanded you."* (Mathew 28:19-20)

I baptized 100 people in India a few years ago. I feel so guilty because I was neither Pastor nor preacher, but I was highly demanded to do. So, I then accepted their request. In the name of Father and our precious pastors here, I really feel guilty until I have read Mathew 28:19-20 concerning the pastor's mission, to make disciples in the name of God. And I understand that this is the way that the Pastor of this church does. As he extends God's disciples to all of us, members of The Capitol Hill Church. The word of God in the sermon of Pastor Jerry simply reminds me of what Pastor Cho said because it is powerful and full of Christian spirits. As the biblical researcher, preacher, and former teacher, I have found that Pastor Cho is everything for Christianity. He is preacher, youth counselor, friend, father, husband, prayer, home visitor, food delivery man, etc. I can say that because he brought his soup to my mother-in-law for all 5 days in the hospital before she passed away. He has followed Jesus's path in feeding the last meal. He is a good sample of the people; even doctors and nurses at the hospital have asked who is that man with, full of love, shine of dignity. Many of them thought that he would be me or one of Dorothy's sons-in-law. Yes, he is. He is in his spirit. He can be everything that we think. Because God gives him unlimited work to serve us, and he follows it with his great will. He is a good samaritan and also mailman, as he loves to send birthday cards and anniversary cards with the Korean tea to everyone, and he does not forget to do it each year. He has a lot to do to serve the Lord. But he didn't feel any difficulty, or it will make him busy. He's still humble, full of joy and delight to do everything. He is someone we want to be with. He is a clear-minded person, understands the meaning of God's word quickly and very well and he can explain clearly for us to understand. For example, he explained that the Cross is not only a symbol of Christianity but also the symbol of Jesus. We have to remember him appreciate him for his hard work to us no matter what time. He does his day and night working beyond his contract that assigned him to go extra miles, far away from his homeland. He has to deal with many issues of the Church and community here and in other nations. He helped raise fund for the Flu for Asian countries. He took other's problems as his own. When he heard that someone has been sick, he was always there and let us know. When someone passed away, he was there to comfort his / her family and helped manage everything until the funeral ceremony is completed.

Even he is leaving us for somewhere else, but he will be remembered, always in our hearts. Everything he did will be a good memory we will never forget especially the word of God he has delivered to us. Let me add a little more thing that I will never forget, when my mother-in-law passed away, I called him, and five minutes later, he was there for me, for my wife, for my family. It's something I'm very, very grateful for. When we need him, he is there! What more do we need from him or expect from him. Anytime he is being need, he immediately did it, and he has done the same thing to everyone. I, personally, deeply admire him and appreciate all his works he has done.

Pray that we will able to have someone like him to our church, the Capitol Hill Church.

Capitol Hill Church United Methodist Church Portland, Oregon

THE AUTHOR'S ADDRESS ON THE WEDDING OCCASION OF DONA DUMDEANG, HIS DAUGHTER, AND JEN POWELL

AT TULUM BEACH, MEXICO CITY

On May 6, 1977, at the St. Louis Hospital in Bangkok, Thailand, our beautiful and lovely daughter was born. My wife named her Dona, Anintra Dumdeang. It was the happiest day of my wife and me because we have had our gorgeous and beautiful living creature of our life, Dona, in the World. She is the apple of my eyes. And she had filled my heart with joy and happiness, which I have never felt before. She is my everything, my baby girl, my beautiful girl. She shines brightly amongst the Sun and Moon in the sky and on Earth. Now, she grows up with abundant friends, both men and women at all ages. She loves all of them. Her life was full of love and joy. About 6 years ago, she met her true and eternal love; Jen. It is said that one must learn to love oneself before one can truly love others. And Dona is the example of that saying. She learns how to love herself and gives her true love to her beloved Jen. Based on the Christianism sense of love, "love your neighbor as yourself."

The love that a couple has for each other is a powerful love, graceful love. It is pure and eternal love. Love is miracle, and at the same time, it is mythical from the heart. It is not just a saying phrase, "I love you," but do not really know the meaning of it. But when one says "I love you", it can be seen as just only wording or just the habit to say that according to his/her our culture, but the one who receive or hear the message may appreciate it and interpret in other way. Maybe it's a true declaration of love but in fact, it is a misunderstanding of the receiver only. And this kind of love will not last as it is not a true love. The love of Dona and Jen is not just words according to social etiquette and culture.

But it is the love from their hearts, a love that has a strong and solid foundation, that miraculously brought these two people to be closer together. Their love is beyond any description of love of any religion. Their love is a special reward of their spiritual practices, which help them developing their ability to create love for oneself and for others as well. Real love is not just feeling love or to be loved. Many people who possess a feeling of love or who are in love will act differently, may be constructive or destructive.

But Jen and Dona the have real love, a constructive love. Both of them are both firm in their love for each other. True love is not a feeling which we are overwhelming, but it is a commitment and thoughtful decision to share everything in life together. And all of us have witnessed their love here and today.

If we turn to look at Christianity, which I have chosen to believe and practice, Biblical love is moral character, how we act and treat other human beings. As we are children of God, this character comes from Jesus Christ. *"Dear friends, let us love one another, for love comes from God. Everyone who loves has been born of God and knows God."* (1 John 4:7)

I would love to have someone treating me with kindness, respect, humility, and patience rather than approaching me because I am only attracted to that person. Let me tell you about the definition of the love of God. My wife, Patty, is a real Christian believer and she leads me to believe that "Love is patient, love is kind." It does not envy, it does not boast, it is not provided, It does not dishonor others. It is not self-seeking. It is not easily angered; it keeps no record of wrong. Love does not delight in evil but rejoices with the truth. It always protects, always trust, always hope, always perseveres!! (1Corinthian 13:4-7)

And that is the love that my wife and I we have treated each other since we have been together. It is also the way that we make our relationship with others. And I would like that our kind of love will relate to our daughters and to all of us who are here today. It is my message to all of you, too. *"Love is HOPE for the best for all people."*

With love, the couple will endure everything since the marriage until death never give up ... and that's the way my wife has followed until today. Marriage life is not the easiest thing, but it is not the hardest thing to make it.

There are two theories of love from the place where I came from that touch me. The first one is people who love each other must have loved each other and have been together since the previous life. In this circumstance, their love remains together and will follow each other like a shadow forever. Another theory is that both couple support and take good care of each other. Handing over the good things that are needed by each other until this act becomes love for each other. Both of these two ideas of love are still accepted by Buddhists today. Love is not to control another, but love unites two people into one. There is a saying in the Thai society where I came from that, *"The husband is like the front leg of elephant, leading his wife, which is like the hind leg."* I think if I would out to be the leader as the front leg of the elephant to my wife, our marriage life should not last like this. So I, somehow, don't appreciate my culture, as I have mentioned. I found it very sad. And the women in Thai society seem to accept it ... so terrible. My best friend, Dr. Cook, has studied this subject and he has written a book on it. I have translated it into Thai. But I found that this book has no effect and never ... on Thai marriage culture even today. I have never gotten the answer why our society think about marriage like that.

I like a short love poem saying ...

And that is what my wife has done to me. How lucky I am to be her husband, her smart husband. There is another poem that I would like to share with you today too, saying ... That your eyes tell that you'll love every day.

So does the spiritual love grow ... hand in hand ... Therefore, it is a perfection love.

How suitable spouse are they? We're here to honor, to witness. And to congratulate them. This is the moment of true love which they express to each other. And to the world. They have written their love and real love story today. No one else cannot do it for them. Just only themselves. Their love story has happened since now. And they have shared it with us and with the world. All against gender, abnormal to be normal. It's time to accept the real status of both of them now. It is time to all hidden in the closet to come out."

I as the father of Dona and the new father for Jen, I am very happy and very proud of both of them. Dona always asks me, *"Papa, can you love me as I am?"* No more question, my dear. No matter what you are, I always love the way you are. You are forever my dearest daughter. And all of us who gather together here respect and sincerely accept you and Jen. Even to the stars, moon, sun, or wave from the Ocean and birds in the sky, all nature and super nature here in Tulum are witness and accept both of you too. You are honored as today is your moment my dear daughter. Both of you have true love. As Mahatma Gandhi said that, there is love, there is life. Look at me and my wife; we look after each other each day, and this is the way that Jen and Dona should do the same way. And your marriage will last forever and ever ... I agree with the definitions of love of God because we can take it as a guideline for the foundation of a couple's life. That is how I have built my family with my lovely wife. My love goes to my children, my grandchildren, my friends, and my community. I do love that our dear Dona and Jen will build their life in such a way. Because this will bring you two to a real love, and it will be your love forever and even for your next life. Dona and Jen, both of you were destined to be each other's counterparts from a superpower, and that will also blessed both of you ... the love of everybody here today, including the family of Dumdeang, Powell, Boomer, Madale, Sui, and all friends bless you two, to have happy family. Love is love, it is unmeasurable.

Dona and Jen, don't forget that all of us here; we are family, we have unmeasurable love and friendship ... we are joined together to witness your Wedding here in Tulum, one of the most beautiful beach in the world, where the warm, windy weather, the sound of waves hitting the shore, the singing birds in the slay, are the real natural music to bless both of you too.

The beautiful couple in the white wedding gown clearly reflect the pure white hearts of them that unite together; and signify the miracle which has happened to both of them, to have a special day of life together as they are mean to be soulmate to live together for eternity. Please know that today is another important in the lives of both Dona and Jen, which is very important to me, my wife, Sharon and all of us here too. We unite here to bless them for their super happy day. Thank you for your time and money to travel across the country and the globe (like Boomers and my three sisters from Thailand.) We come to join our child's wedding here, and we're all not the local people from here. What the best!

Don, one of my friend, told me earlier that this wedding is one of the best event in the world and he has enjoyed very much. Dona and Jen have done a great job. Thanks to both of them for inviting Papa and all of us here. How can we forget such a beautiful day and appreciate Dona and Jen.? I have more fun than I expected. It's beyond what I can handle. I have been waiting for this moment for many years.

My daughter, Dona, is full of energy, charming, and manage everything very well. Everyone who know and meet her will love her, and Jen is the one as well. Dona and Jen, they have many things in common; the way they live, the way they see the world, understand and express themselves to manage the world's problems. They both adjust well to everything together. Now, I have another daughter in my life, Jen, who is smart and beautiful, who teaches the children to love the nature, to grow up with wisdom, and to achieve their dream like her. She is now legally a member of our Dumdeang family. How proud, how happy, and how honored I am to be her father-in-law. I don't even know what to say ... I love you, Dona and Jen. Thank you to Sharon for loving our daughter, Dona, and accept her in your family under your wing. She is your daughter now.

One thing I always say to everyone at weddings, even at my recent address for my niece Sara and John's Wedding, is, *"Maintaining a married life is like a struggle. But it is a struggle to find solutions to improve the life of a married couple, a long and stable life forever."* My lovely wife, Patty and me, we have married over 45 years ... Amen ... and we fight and fight for solutions to live together. This technique comes from my father-in-law., Bob, who addressed it to my dear friend, Thai couple, many years ago, and I agreed with him, so I adopted it and have practices since that day. Thanks to Bob to teach us ... so now, I will transfer it to Dona and Jen ... so both of you will live and stay together forever. Now it is the right time for me to invite all of you to bless Dona and Jen. May God and Lord bless both of you and all of us here as well. Thanks again for coming and joining us today, and I wish you all a safe trip back to your home. Thanks to the organization team, musicians, photographers, hair-dresser, and wedding dress designer. You all help making this a beautiful memory day. I should better stop now as there are a few more speakers after me.

Thank you. Amen.

Daney Dumdeang, Father of Dona 12/08/17

TOM'S SPEECH AT THE CAPITOL METHODIST CHURCH

This session concerns about Tom's speech at the Capitol Methodist church. Tom is the author's assistant and co-author of many books.

The author invited Tom to give a talk at the Capitol Methodist church of Portland, Oregon, USA, as he visited the author in the year 2014.

"Rev. Pastor Cho, distinguished members of Capitol Methodist Church.

First of all, please allow me to express my gratitude to Former Pastor Rev. David E. Weekly, who allowed all members of this Church to help raising fund for my wife's medical expenses. She has passed away in peace after being a bedridden patient in my care for 12 years.

My special thank goes to Dr. Daney Dumdeang, my best friend who sponsored me to travel from Thailand to the United States of America and who was also the initiator in fundraising under Rev. David's permission to help me for the funeral of my late wife in Bangkok, Thailand. My special thank also goes to Patty Dumdeang, Daney's wife and permanent member of this church, who introduces me to all of you today.

Dr. Daney Dumdeang and I, we have been friends for over 50 years since both of us were young novices at Wat Mai Phiren, Thonburi, Thailand. Later, we were apart, as I went to study Politics, Finance, and Banking at the University of Negross Occidental Recoletos, a Catholic University in the Republic of Philippines, which is run by the Spanish Catholic Priest. Meanwhile, Dr. Daney go to further his studies in the United States of America. However, we both continued to contact each other ever since.

Let me introduce myself. My name is Intarakiat Rodpradit. My first nickname is Xai, given by my grandfather, which means "boy" on my native language; dialect of North-eastern provinces of Thailand. My second nickname is Pook, given by my late Guru, a famous preacher and the abbot of Wat Borabue, Mahasarakham province, Thailand. And I was named "Tom" by Dr. Daney Dumdeang since I have been here, in the USA.

My ambition since my graduation from the Philippines is to continue my studies and working in the USA. My best friend, Dr. Daney, has hardly contacted and applied for a Social Security Certificate Number to get me here. But it was me. I hesitated and did not come here. Otherwise, I would have lived and studied here a long times ago.

Even though I haven't been in America, I still keep in touch with Dr. Daney, my best friend. One day, Dr Daney informed me that he was writing a book, "The Crisis of 3 Southern Provinces of Thailand." He then invited me to work with him as co-author. I gladly accepted his invitation without hesitation. We enjoyed working together. And the book has already been published. When one of his best friend, Pol. Lt. Jaruek Sam-ang-sri, former high ranking Police Officer of Border Patrol Police Division of Southern Thailand, wanted to come to USA for his medical treatment, but he cannot travel alone according to the problems of his health and his English language. So Dr. Daney has asked me to accompany Pol. Lt. Jaruek to come to the USA. That's the reason why I have been here.

From the story I have just told you, I would like to take this opportunity to express my sincere gratitude to all of you here once again for helping raising funds for my late wife's medical expenses and her funeral.

I wholeheartedly thank you all of you.

Intarakiat Rodpradit

PASTOR EILIDH LOWERY

Eilidh Lowery was born in the European country, Ireland; and moved to the USA with her parents.

She became pastor at Capitol Hill Church a few years after Parter Cho had to move to another church. This church is where my wife and I have attended for over 40 years. Due to a lack of funding and a small number of members, the church did not have enough budget to use for the management, especially to pay for fire insurance. So, it is decided to close the church. And then, Eilidh has been assigned to Trinity Church located at 395 St. Steele, Portland, Oregon, USA.

Eilidh has served this church for over a decade now. My wife and I have also attended this church until the present time. It is very important for me to gain faith in God more and more, as Pastor Eilidh carefully and attentively gives a preach each time. Her sermons are clear and full of faith in Word of God.

When her father passed away, I was the one who went to comfort her. I know that in time of grief, everyone needs encouragement and support. All that I can say to her is that I'm sorry to hear about her loss and hug her.

I told her that now her father is in heaven with our Lord. She was grateful and thank me. We are getting closer.

Thank God we meet.

Parter Eilidh married to Jeff Lowery and has one beautiful and smart daughter who has just graduated from the Cleveland High School this year, 2023. She is accepted at a creditable university in the East. "Eilidh's daughter, Paige, andher husband, Jeff Lowery... Jeff is a man of God. He has children, musician children, and trying to establish helping homeless ministry.

Thank Jeff, for helping our community in Portland to be better living place... Good Job, Jeff... Amen.

In her life, the plays many roles: pastor, wife, mother, VIP at Cleveland High School, and many other organization. She broke her feet while conducting a world business at Cleveland High School. She currently uses a wheelchair to help her walk. Even her feet was broken, she has never missed any service and preaching of the church. She is full of confidence and faith in God. She is honest and believe in her duty to do the mission of God. We are so lucky and happy to have her as our Partner at the church.

May God bless you, Pastor Eilidh Lowery. Thank you for your kindness to preach us and to do the Work of God.

Dr. Daney Dumdeang

The President of the Dumdeang Foundation

Matthew 6:25-33

"Therefore I tell you, do not worry about your life, what you will eat or drink; or about your body, what you will wear. Is not life more than food, and the body more than clothes? 26 Look at the birds of the air; they do not sow or reap or store away in barns, and yet your heavenly Father feeds them. Are you not much more valuable than they? 27 Can any one of you by worrying add a single hour to your life[a]? 28 "And why do you worry about clothes? See how the flowers of the field grow. They do not labor or spin. 29 Yet I tell you that not even Solomon in all his splendor was dressed like one of these. 30 If that is how God clothes the grass of the field, which is here today and tomorrow is thrown into the fire, will he not much more clothe you—you of little faith? 31 So do not worry, saying, 'What shall we eat?' or 'What shall we drink?' or 'What shall we wear?' 32 For the pagans run after all these things, and your heavenly Father knows that you need them. 33 But seek first his kingdom and his righteousness, and all these things will be given to you as well.

This is the word of God for the people of God. Thanks be to God!

Death never seems to come on time. For some, it comes too early, and for others, it comes too late. One truth about death we know is it is always sudden and frustrating. Even if it's been expected for a while, it comes quick, suddenly, and unpredictably. It comes along with an emotional mixture: sorrow, anger, despair, anxiety, and emptiness.

We heard her breathe, we saw her eyes move under the eyelids while sleeping, and we felt her warmth by touching smoothly and lovingly on her arms. And suddenly, we realized she was not there anymore. Death snatched her away from us. We become totally overwhelmed by this unmanageable event in life. She couldn't be with the family for the Thanksgiving dinner anymore. Everything may seem different to the family in this season of joy and gratitude.

I know Dorothy has been a wonderful grandma to many of you. Spending several hours with the family at the hospital while Dorothy was agonizing and groaning in pain, I could see how much they loved and cared about her. If they could, they wouldn't let her go. The family truly worried about her. And now there seems to be another worry rising up about the future for the family. What now without such a lovely mother and grandma? Who would make all the family stick to each other?

Then, we hear from Jesus, *"Do not worry. Do not worry about anything."*

Does this word really convince and comfort us while we're all grieving for the loss of this good friend? It doesn't seem making any sense. And we may want to ask Jesus, *"If we shouldn't worry, then what are we supposed to do?"* The Bible teaches us very clearly about this. WE SHOULD BE THANKFUL!

It is paradox. While having something to worry about, we gotta be thankful instead. While our heart is broken and grieving, yet, we hear the Lord say, we should be thankful. How can it be possible?

It is possible. I know it is very hard to understand sometimes. But it is true. We should be thankful this moment because we know our dear friend, Dorothy, doesn't have to suffer and scream in pain anymore. Death released her from pain and delivered her into the hand of God, who gives true peace and rest.

And we're thankful for the time God has granted us to enjoy with Dorothy. While the time seemed plenty, we hardly realized it was special gift of God. This is our stupidity as human beings. We often waste our time and miss opportunities to show our love to our loving friends and family when they live close to us. Do not waste your time. Do not wait till tomorrow. Show your love now and say you love them!

I believe it was Dorothy's gift for the family to get them together in the hospital and remind them of her love. The family will remember the last week of Dorothy through their lives. It was very short, but it was intensive and meaningful. I would say even though the family flew and drove over to the hospital and shared their wisdom to do something good for Dorothy, the moments were for them. Dorothy was touching in their hearts and nourishing and comforting by staying with them there with her best.

That is mom's heart. God raises up all his wonderful creatures through the hands of parents. The only way we can taste of God's unconditional love is through our parents. Dorothy, until the very last moment, I believe, truly cared for her children and grandchildren and all her loving friends. We are thankful for this love.

We, Christians, are yet to be thankful because we know we will meet again. We're heading towards one same place. In this hope for the resurrection, despite the separation of Dorothy from all of us, we look forwards to seeing and meeting with her again. That becomes a reason for us to be thankful. I'd like to share a poem which seems perfectly fit in this moment. Daney wanted to share this with all of you in this moment of celebration of the life of Dorothy:

Again, I tell you, all family and friends. Dorothy is not dead as long as you remember her smiling face in your heart, as long as you live on all the good memories, stories about her, and as long as you hold on to this faith of our resurrection. Are you thankful for her? Yes, we are.

May the love and healing grace of God be with you all now and forever more.

Amen.